Three Sisters Bake

December 12, 2014

Dear Jennifer,

    As the welcome to this cookbook says, we "love talking about food, tasting it, experimenting with it and reading about it"! So, although neither you or I have a sister, we can relate; I know.

    We are thrilled to count you as a member of our Berg family. Lucky us! ♡

Happy Birthday! Best wishes!

        Love,
        Sue and Greg
        XX OO

Three Sisters Bake

Delectable Recipes for Every Day

GILLIAN, NICHOLA AND LINSEY REITH

hardie grant books

MELBOURNE · LONDON

Contents

Welcome to Three Sisters Bake

We are three sisters obsessed with food. We love talking about it, tasting it, experimenting with it and reading about it. We never tire of the stuff.

You could say that our love affair with food is hereditary. With a home economics teacher for a mother and grandparents who owned a sweetie shop, we were perhaps headed for a life of food from the outset.

In 2011, we turned our food daydreams into a reality and opened the doors of our café, Three Sisters Bake, in Quarriers Village in the Scottish countryside. We set out with a meager budget and grand plans; to create an oasis of food, caffeine, calm and countryside air. Nowadays, we're delighted to welcome visitors from all over Scotland to the café in addition to our close-knit group of local customers (including our very own knitting group).

We take a great deal of inspiration from our idyllic village location. We also take pride in using local ingredients whenever possible and enjoy taking a traditional Scottish dish and adding a Three Sisters Bake twist. Our Tattie Scone Stack made with home-baked potato scones and Stornoway black pudding (page 28) is one of the most popular breakfast dishes on our menu.

Our philosophy has always been to 'delight the senses'. We like our food to look as good as it tastes. We wanted the recipes in this book to be a reflection of the type of food we serve in the café and also the food we eat at home: simple, innovative, everyday food made with fresh, wholesome ingredients. Oh, and lots of cakes!

We hope you enjoy making them as much as we do.

Where it all began...

We were brought up in a house warmed by cooking smells, home baking and breads from the Aga. Our childhood memories invariably involve craft projects, creating sculptures from homemade play dough and learning to make traybakes at the kitchen table.

Our granny and grandpa owned an old-fashioned sweetie shop in a little village in Scotland called Kirriemuir. As children, visiting them was like Charlie being taken to the chocolate factory. We would spend hours standing on a stool behind the tall counter helping to serve customers, dropping colourful sweets into paper bags and counting coins at the old cash register. As well as jar upon jar of sweets, Granny also sold her own homemade 'tablet' (a traditional Scottish sweet, with the consistency of a slightly crumbly fudge). Granny's tablet was so popular that she made a full tray every day, which she cut into small squares and portioned into little bags. We were often given jobs on the tablet production line to keep us out of mischief! Nowadays, when people ask what made us want to open a café, I'm sure that watching the fascinating process of Granny making and selling tablet had a lot to do with it.

We were given our first real taste of the hospitality industry as teenagers, when we went to work in our local coffee shop. We slowly learned the art of cappuccino making, under the watchful eye of our boss and mentor Liz, and we watched in awe as she single-handedly ran a kitchen, manned the coffee machine, managed paperwork and charmed her army of loyal customers. She made it look so easy!

Anyone who has ever worked in a café, kitchen, restaurant, hotel or bar will tell you that it is hard work, but also great fun. It really gets under your skin and becomes part of who you are. Looking back, it's obvious that the allure of the hospitality industry had already begun to seep into each of us, even at that young age.

We all left school and went off into the world. I studied English at Strathclyde University, Nichola headed for studies at Aberdeen University's science department and Linsey followed Nichola to Aberdeen University to study English.

Like most graduates, we had no idea what we wanted from life, so we independently set off in search of adventure. We each spent the next few years working our way around the world; waitressing in cafés and restaurants, cooking on luxury yachts and in ski chalets, working in beach resorts and pulling pints of Guinness in Irish bars.

Along the way, we found time to pursue and explore our passion for food. We consumed the fluffiest of pancakes in New York, the most exquisite Sauvignon Blanc in New Zealand, cupcakes that looked too good to eat in San Francisco and freshly caught fish in Croatia. For a short time, Linsey lived opposite a boulangerie in France and sampled every pastry and tart on offer, while Nichola and I lived and worked in Australia, experiencing Melbourne's enviable café culture, gourmet brunch menus and the Aussie obsession with excellent coffee. Although plans to open a café of our own were still far away, we must have been subconsciously storing ideas, inspiration and flavours to call upon in the years to come.

Eventually, we all realised we must return home, to the real world and to 'grown-up' jobs. I spent a number of years working in PR and marketing, Nichola worked as a project manager with a pharmaceutical company and Linsey in Human Resources. Our combined interest in food, coffee, wine and café culture was temporarily smothered under files, emails and administration.

However, the sensible 'proper' jobs weren't to last and, one by one, we began to hear the call of the hospitality industry. We escaped our dull desk jobs, lured back to the helter skelter world of restaurants and cooking: Nichola worked as a baker, Linsey trained as a chef, and I worked front of house in a café in Glasgow's West End.

It didn't take long before the idea of opening a café of our own began to firmly take root. We would meet up for tapas and a glass of wine every week, bursting with ideas about menus, logo design, business plans, potential locations, names for our café and its décor. Every detail was pored over, right down to what colour the salt and pepper mills should be!

After months and months of looking, we eventually found a suitable premises to launch our café business. The terrifying process of turning our dreams into a reality began to take shape as we knocked down walls, painted doors, built furniture and filled the shelves with produce. Eventually, in October 2011, we were ready to open our doors.

Since then we have had a rollercoaster time of it as our family has grown both at the café and at home. We have recruited staff who have become integral members of the Three Sisters Bake team. We've made firm friends with many of our local customers and have started a weekly knitting group and 'Baby Social' group. We've also squeezed in some maternity leave; I had a little girl, Rosie, in 2012 and Nichola had baby Tate in 2013!

Although we have a great team working with us now, we are all still actively involved in the running of the café. Nichola heads up our wedding cake business, Linsey manages our outside catering orders and I look after our food truck and events.

As for the future, who knows what is in store at Three Sisters Bake... We don't rest on our laurels for long and can't wait for the next phase of the adventure to begin!   GILLIAN

Brunch

At Three Sisters Bake, breakfast is not only the most important meal of the day, it is also the most exciting!

As sisters, we often get asked how we manage to work together without falling out. The truth is, while we do have the odd disagreement, when it comes to the important things, we always seem to agree. We have very similar outlooks on life, business and, most importantly, food. One of these being that we all LOVE, cherish and adore breakfast time.

We can often go through a busy day at the café without seeing one another very much, but the one time of day we always spend together is breakfast. We were brought up to eat breakfast as a family at the kitchen table, even if it was just a five minute stop on the way to the school bus. Our breakfasts invariably consisted of cereal, toast or porridge.

It was not until we started travelling after university and all independently ventured to Australia that our eyes were opened to the full potential of breakfast as a truly exciting meal. Anyone who has ever visited Australia will testify that the café culture is quite phenomenal. Every tiny café in the suburbs of Sydney and Melbourne seems to have the most exciting and innovative brunch menus.

Growing up in Scotland, the extent of our experience of breakfast menus was bacon rolls or a full fried breakfast. Our eyes popped out of our heads when faced with menus full of homemade granolas, stacks of pancakes with berries, maple syrup, bacon and bananas, rainbow-coloured tropical fruit salads, fresh yoghurt, corn cakes, poached eggs with avocado, smoothies and juices containing every fruit imaginable and, of course, amazing coffee!

People return from Australia full of a love of food and great coffee or with a burning desire to open their own coffee shop and claim a piece of Aussie-inspired café culture for themselves. That is certainly what happened to us. The recipes in this chapter reflect the huge influence of our travels in Australia while incorporating a number of signature Scottish flavours and ingredients. NICHOLA

Blueberry Pancake Stack

The pancake stack must be the dictionary definition of decadent breakfasting. What could be better than eating sweet treats first thing in the morning? Surely life doesn't get much more exciting than a Sunday brunch of towering pancakes drizzled with whatever takes your fancy. I've chosen my favourite topping – blueberry compote. GILLIAN

SERVES 4

FOR THE BLUEBERRY COMPOTE
200 g (7 oz) blueberries, rinsed
3 tablespoons caster (superfine) sugar

FOR THE PANCAKES
200 g (7 oz/1⅔ cups) plain (all-purpose) flour
1½ teaspoons baking powder
½ teaspoon salt
50 g (2 oz/¼ cup) caster (superfine) sugar
200 ml (7 fl oz) whole (full-cream) milk
2 large eggs, at room temperature, lightly beaten
50 g (2 oz) unsalted butter, melted, plus 15 g (½ oz) for cooking

First, make the blueberry compote. Heat the blueberries, sugar and 1 tablespoon of water in a pan on a very low heat and simmer for 3 minutes. Set aside and allow to cool a little.

To make the pancakes, sift the flour, baking powder, salt and sugar into a bowl.

In a separate bowl whisk the milk and eggs together then whisk in the melted butter.

Pour the wet ingredients into the dry ingredients and whisk together using an electric hand mixer.

Heat a non-stick frying pan on a medium heat and add the remaining butter.

Once melted add a small ladle of the batter. When you start to see bubbles on the top of the pancake, flip it over and cook the other side until golden brown. Repeat until all the batter is used up.

Serve the pancakes in a stack drizzled with the blueberry compote.

Ham Hock and Mature Cheddar Muffins

These yummy muffins are a doddle to make. They're a great breakfast treat to serve up to guests, and there's no need to tell them how simple they are to make! NICHOLA

MAKES 12

EQUIPMENT:
12-hole muffin tin
12 muffin cases (optional)

250 g (9 oz/2 cups) self-raising flour
1 teaspoon baking powder
½ teaspoon bicarbonate of soda (baking soda)
¼ teaspoon salt
125 g (4½ oz) mature Cheddar cheese, grated
100 g (3½ oz) cooked ham hock, diced
90 ml (3 fl oz) sunflower oil, plus a little extra for greasing
150 g (5 oz) natural yoghurt
125 ml (4 fl oz/⅔ cup) whole (full-cream) milk
1 large egg, at room temperature

Preheat the oven to 200°C (400°F/Gas 6). Grease the muffin tin or line with muffin cases.

Sift together the flour, baking powder, bicarbonate of soda and salt.

In a separate bowl, mix the cheese, ham, oil, yoghurt, milk and egg.

Combine the wet ingredients with the dry ingredients using a freestanding mixer or a wooden spoon until well mixed. Divide between the muffin cases or spoon directly into the muffin tin if not using cases.

Bake in the oven for 20 minutes until golden and cooked through. Remove and leave to cool slightly on a wire rack.

Halloumi and Chipotle Mayo Mini Cornbread Sandwich

An alternative, fiery brunch favourite at Three Sisters Bake.

MAKES 4 SANDWICHES

1 quantity Homemade Mayo (page 131)

2 dried chipotle chillies, seeded

2 tablespoons roughly chopped coriander (cilantro)

grated zest of 1 lime

1 tablespoon rapeseed oil

250 g (9 oz) pack of halloumi cheese, sliced lengthways into ½-cm- (¼-in-) wide strips

4 American-style Cornbread Muffins (page 121)

40 g (1½ oz) rocket (arugula) leaves, to serve

Make the mayo adding the chipotle chillies, coriander and lime at the end. Whizz well to combine. You should end up with a lovely vivid orange, spicy mayo.

Meanwhile, heat the oil in a non-stick griddle pan on a high heat. When the griddle is very hot, add the halloumi slices, sear for 1–2 minutes on each side, until each one has golden brown charred lines. Remove from the griddle pan and set aside.

Slice through the middle of each cornbread muffin. Spread one side of each muffin with a generous spoonful of chipotle mayo, top with rocket followed by charred halloumi, and top each with the remaining muffin halves.

Banana Bread

This is another one of our recipes inspired by my time in Australia. Every café worth its salt in Oz sells this treat, toasted and slathered in butter. When my husband and I lived there he ate banana bread for breakfast every day for six months… all the while refusing to admit that he started every day with cake! Sorry dear, it may have bread in the title but this is most definitely a cake. NICHOLA

SERVES 10

EQUIPMENT:
900 g (2 lb) loaf tin

350 g (12 oz/1½ cups) caster (superfine) sugar
110 g (3½ oz) unsalted butter, at room temperature, plus extra for greasing
2 large eggs, at room temperature
225 g (8 oz/1¾ cups) plain (all-purpose) flour
¼ teaspoon baking powder
½ teaspoon bicarbonate of soda (baking soda)
3 large over-ripe bananas, peeled and flesh mashed
1 teaspoon vanilla extract
75 g (2½ oz/½ cup) nuts or seeds (optional)
handful of chocolate drops or blueberries (optional)

Preheat the oven to 180°C (350°F/Gas 4). Lightly grease and line the tin with greaseproof (wax) paper.

Beat the sugar and butter for 3–4 minutes until soft and fluffy. Add the eggs one at a time, beating continuously. Sift the flour, baking powder and bicarbonate of soda into the mixture and fold in. Now stir in the mashed bananas and vanilla extract. Add the nuts or seeds, chocolate drops or blueberries at this stage, if using.

Pour the mixture into the prepared loaf tin and bake in the oven for 1 hour 15 minutes. Check if it's ready by inserting a skewer into the centre of the bread – if it does not come out clean, return it to the oven for another 10 minutes.

Let the banana bread cool completely before turning it out of the tin. Serve sliced, toasted with butter. and enjoy for breakfast, lunch or dinner!

Boston Beans on Rye

Boston beans started off on our Soul BBQ menu at Three Sisters Bake,
but have become a real firm favourite on the Brunch menu specials, too.
The pancetta gives this dish just an edge of smokiness, but you can skip
it for a veggie alternative. This won't come as a surprise: we urge you
to try it topped with mature Scottish Cheddar for the classic,
fantastic cheesy beano! GILLIAN

SERVES 4

1 teaspoon vegetable oil
100 g (3½ oz) smoked pancetta, cubed
1 white onion, diced
1 garlic clove, crushed
1 stick of celery, diced
1 green (bell) pepper, halved, stalk removed,
    seeded and diced
120 g (4 oz/½ cup) soft, dark brown sugar
400 g (14 oz) tin of chopped tomatoes
1 teaspoon smoked paprika
1 teaspoon ground cumin
pinch of Chinese five spice
3 cloves
2 × 400 g (14 oz) tins of cannellini beans,
    drained and rinsed
pinch of salt and cracked black pepper
4 slices of Rye and Raisin Bread (page 115)

Heat the oil in a heavy-based pan on a high
heat. Add the pancetta and fry for 5 minutes
until it is crispy. Add the onion, garlic, celery
and green pepper and fry, stirring continually,
until the vegetables are soft but not browned.
Add the sugar, chopped tomatoes and spices.

Turn the heat down and simmer for 10 minutes,
or until the mixture has reduced by a third.
Add the cannellini beans and season to taste.

Toast the bread, top it with the beans and serve
straight away.

Tattie Scone Stack

This hangover-friendly dish involves a couple of our favourite Scottish breakfast staples: black pudding and potato scones. Stornoway black pudding is seriously worth spending a little more money on if you can get it. Everyone has their own knack to the perfect poached egg. Mine is a good glug of vinegar, a deep pot of water and a cooking time of three minutes. LINSEY

SERVES 4

4 large cooking apples, such as Bramley
1 tablespoon olive oil
30 g (1 oz) salted butter
30 g (1 oz/⅙ cup) caster (superfine) sugar
400 g (14 oz) Stornoway black pudding, sliced into 1-cm- (½-in-) thick pieces
4 slices of Sourdough Bread (page 117)
1 tablespoon vegetable oil
4 Tattie Scones (page 120)
2 tablespoons clear malt vinegar
4 large eggs
70 g (2 ¼ oz) rocket (arugula) leaves

Preheat the oven to 120°C (250°F/Gas ½). Quarter and core the cooking apples (no need to peel them). Cut each quarter into 4 slices.

Heat the oil and butter in a non-stick frying pan. Add the apple slices and cook on a medium heat, stirring every minute or so. When the apples are softening a little but still firm, sprinkle over the sugar. Cook for another 2 minutes, until the sugar has dissolved and the apples are caramelizing. Remove from heat.

Arrange the black pudding slices on a baking tray and cook in the oven for 15 minutes.

Bring a large pan of water to the boil.

At this point timing can get a little hectic – 5 minutes before the black pudding is due to come out of the oven, put the sourdough slices in the toaster. Remove them before they are fully toasted and transfer to a baking tray and heat in the oven. Place apples on a heatproof plate and pop in to the oven.

Heat the vegetable oil in a non-stick frying pan on a medium heat for one minute. Fry the tattie scones for 1–2 minutes on each side, until lightly golden. Transfer these to the oven, or to a warm plate.

Add the vinegar to the pan of boiling water and turn the heat down to a gentle simmer. Crack the eggs into the water, one quickly after another. Set your timer for 3 minutes.

You now have 3 minutes to remove everything from the oven (while the eggs are cooking), and plate up a stack of rocket, topped with sourdough toast, tattie scone, black pudding and caramelized apple on 4 plates.

When the timer goes, remove the poached eggs from the pan with a slotted spoon. Tip any excess water off the eggs and carefully drain them on a tea towel or some kitchen roll. Top each stack with one poached egg and serve straight away.

Agave-Poached Peaches with Toasted Brazil Nut Granola

Most shop-bought granolas or breakfast cereals are full of sugar and oils. We did a lot of playing around with this granola combination to come up with something which is as convenient and quick as the boxed equivalent, but tastes SO much better and doesn't rely on a pile of unhealthy additives. LINSEY

SERVES 6

6 ripe peaches
100 ml (3½ fl oz) agave syrup
grated zest and juice of 1 unwaxed lemon

FOR THE GRANOLA
40 g (1½ oz) brazil nuts, roughly chopped
30 g (1 oz) pistachios, roughly chopped
30 g (1 oz) blanched almonds, roughly chopped
30 g (1 oz) unsweetened coconut, shredded
20 g (¾ oz/scant ¼ cup) jumbo oats
40 g (1½ oz/ ⅓ cup) dried cranberries
40 g (1½ oz/ ⅓ cup) raisins

500 g (1 lb 2 oz) Greek yoghurt, to serve

Leaving the peaches whole, put them in a medium-sized pan and add enough water to nearly cover them. Add the agave syrup, lemon zest and juice to the pan and bring to a simmer on a medium heat. Simmer gently for 15 minutes, carefully turning the peaches once or twice. The liquid should reduce a little and thicken. Remove the pan from the heat, take the peaches out of the liquid and allow to cool. Reserve the poaching juices.

Preheat the oven to 160°C (320°F/Gas 2).

To make the granola, combine the chopped nuts with the coconut, oats and dried fruit on a large flat baking tray. Drizzle 150 ml (5 fl oz) of the peach poaching juices over the dry granola mix (just add enough to lightly coat). Toss the granola ingredients to coat everything in the juices.

Bake the granola mix for 10 minutes, then rake it through with a fork and bake for a further 10 minutes. Continue to do this, checking at regular intervals, until the oats, nuts and fruit are golden and crisping up. Remove the tray from the oven and set aside to cool. As it cools, the granola will solidify and crisp up further, giving it a really nice crunch.

Serve each peach in a bowl with a generous spoonful of yoghurt and top with granola.

Love Eggs

*A super healthy, veggie friendly breakfast – it's the
Mother Teresa of breakfasts!*

SERVES 4

FOR THE SALSA

8 large ripe vine tomatoes

1 large red bell pepper, halved, stem removed
and deseeded

1 red onion

small handful of coriander (cilantro)

juice of 1 lime

3 tablespoons extra virgin olive oil

10 jalapeno slices (from a jar), depending
on taste (optional)

1 teaspoon clear malt vinegar

4 large eggs

4 slices of Sourdough Bread (page 117)

1 ripe avocado

First make the salsa. Finely chop the tomatoes,
red pepper, onion and coriander and mix
together in a bowl. Add the lime juice and olive
oil and stir through. Add the jalapenos at this
point, if you like your salsa with a kick!

Bring a large pan of water to the boil and add
the vinegar. Once the water has come to the
boil break the eggs into a small bowl or cup
and, one at a time, quickly slide them into the
water. Cook for 2–3 minutes. To test if they are
ready, lift an egg out with a slotted spoon and
gently touch it – the white should be firm and
the yolk still soft to the touch.

While the eggs are cooking toast the sourdough
and prepare the avocado – remove the skin and
stone and chop the flesh into slices.

Finally, assemble everything – place 1 piece of
toast on each plate, then lay the avocado slices
on top of the toast, followed by the eggs, then
a generous spoon of salsa to finish.

Scrambled Eggs Coogee Style

I used to eat a similar breakfast to this in a café in the Sydney beachside suburb of Coogee. I may not have a sea view while eating it these days but it still tastes great! The key to good scrambled eggs is to cook them very slowly and watch them like a hawk. Get all your ingredients ready and laid out before you put the eggs on to cook. NICHOLA

SERVES 2

FOR THE RED ONION MARMALADE
1 tablespoon extra virgin olive oil
15 g (½ oz) unsalted butter
4 red onions, halved and sliced as thinly
   as possible (ideally use the thinnest blade
   of a food processor or a mandoline)
2 tablespoons dark brown soft sugar
pinch of salt

a handful of pine nuts (pine kernels)
4 large eggs
a knob of unsalted butter
1 tablespoon vegetable oil
2 slices of Sourdough Bread (page 117)
2 handfuls of rocket (arugula) leaves, to serve

First make the red onions marmalade. Heat the oil with the butter in a heavy-based pan on a medium heat. Once the butter has melted add the sliced onions to the pan and cook, stirring to ensure they do not stick, for at least 10–15 minutes, until they are very soft and beginning to brown.

Preheat the oven to 160°C (320°F/Gas 2).

Sprinkle the onions with the sugar and salt and stir. Cook them for a further 5 minutes, continually stirring, until they are caramelized and sticky. Remove from heat and allow to cool completely.

Place the pine nuts on a baking tray and bake in the oven for 3–4 minutes, or until golden brown.

For the scrambled eggs, break the eggs into a bowl and whisk. Melt the butter and oil in a non-stick frying pan over a low heat. When the butter starts bubbling, pour in the eggs. Stir every 10 seconds with a wooden spoon.

While keeping an eye on the eggs, toast the sourdough. Once toasted place a slice on a plate and spread them with the red onion marmalade.

Take your scrambled eggs off the heat just before they are ready (softly set and still a bit runny), as they will continue to cook even once removed from the heat.

Top each piece of sourdough with scrambled egg and garnish with a handful of rocket leaves and a sprinkling of toasted pine nuts.

Kids Hot Jammy Piece

'Piece' is a Scottish word for sandwich. The 'Jeely Piece Song', whose lyrics begin 'Oh ye canna fling pieces oot a twenty storey flat', is known by children across the country and the jam sandwich which inspired the song is a hugely popular snack among Scottish school kids. Here is a slightly more decadent version of the old classic. GILLIAN

SERVES 1

1 tablespoon good-quality raspberry jam
(even better, homemade!)
2 slices of white bread
1 large egg
pinch of salt
dash of double (heavy) cream
a knob of unsalted butter
25 g (1 oz) granulated sugar, for sprinkling

Spread the jam onto one slice of bread. Place the other slice of bread on top to create a jam sandwich. Beat the egg in a small bowl with the salt and a dash of cream.

Melt the butter in a small non-stick frying pan on a medium-high heat. Dip both sides of the sandwich into the egg mixture until all the mixture has been soaked up by the bread.

Fry the sandwich in the pan until it is golden brown on both sides. Make sure it is cooked through before removing it from pan.

Sprinkle both sides of the sandwich liberally with sugar while the sandwich is still hot (this will help the sugar to stick and form a sweet crust).

Homemade Pink Lemonade

This homemade lemonade is the ultimate thirst quencher on a warm morning and can be thrown together in no time. Turn it into an impressive drink for entertaining in the garden by garnishing with lots of lemon, raspberry and mint and serving it in a big jug.

LINSEY

MAKES 6 GLASSES

9 unwaxed lemons
200 g (7 oz/ 1½ cups) fresh raspberries
220 g (7½ oz/1 cup) caster (superfine) sugar
ice cubes, to serve

Zest and juice the lemons.

Place 180 g (6 oz) of the raspberries in a tall jug, add enough water to cover the raspberries and blend with a hand blender.

Mix the lemon juice and zest, sugar and puréed raspberries with 1½ litres (50¾ fl oz) of boiling water.

Leave the mixture to cool, then pour it through a sieve into a large jug (using a wooden spoon to push the liquid through).

Top the lemonade with the remaining raspberries and stir. Serve in glasses filled with ice.

Salads

Like every student, I went off to university (in Aberdeen) and had a ridiculously unhealthy diet for the first couple of years. Our halls of residence served up a stream of deep-fried nondescript food and invariably most of our nights out would end with a portion of chips and cheese (the ultimate 2am snack). My flatmate and I would embark on half-hearted 'health kicks' which involved eating rice with chilli sauce for two nights running before returning to the deep-fried halls fare. It is fair to say I found healthy eating something of a chore!

This all changed the year after I graduated, when I landed a summer job as a stewardess aboard a luxury yacht based in the French port town of Antibes. The head chef on the yacht, Flossy, noticed my growing interest in cooking as I peered over her shoulder every evening, and took me under her wing for the duration of the summer.

As we travelled from port to port across the Mediterranean, she invited me to accompany her on trips to food markets as she shopped for ingredients. We visited the most amazing markets in Capri, all along the Sardinian coast and in small French towns away from the glitz and glamour of St Tropez. The food was like nothing I had ever seen before: piles of colourful shiny vegetables, huge red beef tomatoes, bright yellow and pink furry-skinned peaches, pretty courgette (zucchini) flowers, melons of all shapes and sizes, drums of fresh mozzarella and speckled farm eggs complete with feathers stuck to them. The fish markets brimmed with langoustine, lobster, clams, and fish I'd never even heard of before.

Lunch on board the yacht was a daily celebration. The guests were treated to mountains of freshly baked breads, cold meats, cheeses, seafood and a salad piled high with fresh vegetables. It was the perfect meal to combat the heat of the Mediterranean summer.

From then on, I was hooked. On food, on cooking and on creating delicious, colourful salads. Finally, I understood that eating healthy, nutritious food could be enjoyable! I believe the key to a great salad is simple: experimentation, amazing local produce and fresh vegetables. Have a go!

LINSEY

Watermelon, Feta and Mint Salad

This is a summery twist on a classic Greek salad. We always throw it together as an accompaniment to barbecued lamb but it would be just as good served with a simple chicken dish.

SERVES 6–8

½ small watermelon, flesh cut into 2.5-cm-
(1-in-) cubes

½ cucumber, cut into 1-cm- (½-in-) cubes

200 g (7 oz) feta cheese, cut into 1-cm-
(½-in-) cubes

3 sprigs of mint, leaves picked

100 g (3½ oz) pitted black olives

1 quantity of Charred Orange and Olive Oil
Dressing (page 104)

Combine the watermelon, cucumber and feta cubes, the mint leaves and black olives in a large serving bowl. Stir through enough dressing to coat the salad, and serve.

Barley and Blueberry Salad

In general I'm a massive fan of local produce and try to use it as much as possible in our menu. While most commonly found in the traditional Scotch Broth, I've given it a contemporary twist in this bright, summery salad. Out of the soup pot, the barley lends a lovely bite here, acting as a perfect backdrop for bold blueberries and butternut squash.

LINSEY

SERVES 6–8

400 g (14 oz/1¾ cups) pearl barley
1 medium butternut squash (pumpkin), cut into quarters lengthways (skin on), seeds removed and sliced into 1-cm- (½-in-) pieces
2 tablespoons olive oil
10 pieces of tender stem broccoli, base of stems removed
75 g (2½ oz/½ cup) pine nuts (pine kernels)
100 g (3½ oz/⅔ cup) blueberries (a small punnet), rinsed and drained on kitchen towel
1 quantity of House Dressing (page 105)
salt and freshly ground black pepper

Preheat the oven to 180°C (350°F/Gas 4).

Cook the barley as per the packet instructions, then drain and set aside to cool.

Place the squash pieces in a deep roasting tin, toss with the oil and season. Roast in the oven for 30 minutes or until the squash is tender, tossing the pieces halfway through the cooking time. Remove and set aside to cool.

Meanwhile, steam or boil the broccoli stems for 3–4 minutes. Drain, if necessary, and set aside to cool.

Place the pine nuts on a baking sheet. Bake in the oven for 2 minutes, remove and toss them, then return to the oven. Continue to bake for another 5 minutes, until the pine nuts are a light golden toasted colour. Set aside to cool.

In a big serving bowl, combine the cooked barley, butternut squash, broccoli, pine nuts and blueberries. Drizzle over the dressing. Mix thoroughly and serve.

Summer Rice Salad

We tried not to steal too many recipes from our mum's battered and well- loved recipe box in the creation of this book, but her rice salad just had to feature. She swears that the key is cooking the rice to perfection, as per her directions here. It's just not summer in our house without this.

SERVES 6

1 teaspoon salt
300 g (10½ oz/1½ cups) basmati rice, rinsed
    thoroughly and drained
130 g (4½ oz/1 cup) frozen sweetcorn
130 g (4½ oz/1 cup) frozen peas
3 spring onions (scallions), thinly sliced
1 red (bell) pepper, halved, stalk removed,
    seeded and finely diced
200 g (7 oz/1½ cups) roasted, salted cashew nuts
150 g (5 oz) small cooked prawns

FOR THE DRESSING
200 ml (7 fl oz) extra virgin olive oil
25 ml (1 fl oz) white balsamic vinegar
½ teaspoon English mustard powder
salt and coarsely ground black pepper, to taste

Bring a large pan of water to the boil. Add the salt then the rice and simmer gently for 20 minutes (or cook according to packet instructions).

Meanwhile, put the dressing ingredients in a bowl and whisk well to combine.

Drain the cooked rice and, while it is still warm, spread it out on a flat baking sheet and drizzle over the dressing. Leave to cool.

Cook the sweetcorn and peas in a pan of simmering water for 5 minutes, then drain and set aside to cool.

Combine the dressed rice, vegetables, cashew nuts and prawns in a large salad bowl and serve.

Thai Carrot Salad

This is my light, healthy and slightly more exotic take on coleslaw.
Six ingredients, one glorious punchy dish. LINSEY

SERVES 4–6

50 g (2 oz/⅓ cup) sesame seeds
¾ red chilli (chile), seeded (optional) and
    finely diced
150 ml (5 fl oz) light coconut milk
grated zest and juice of 1 lime
400 g (14 oz) grated carrot
3 tablespoons chopped coriander (cilantro)

Preheat the oven to 180°C (350°F/Gas 4).

Spread the sesame seeds on a baking tray and toast in the oven for 6–8 minutes until they are golden brown and giving off a nutty aroma. Set aside to cool.

In the meantime, make the dressing by combining the chilli, coconut milk, lime zest and juice.

Mix the grated carrot with the chopped coriander and toasted sesame seeds. Add the dressing to the carrot mixture and mix thoroughly.

Roast Pepper and Raisin Couscous

There's a lot going on in this dish with warmth from the spices, fruity raisins and sweetness from the peppers. This makes it a great accompaniment to very simple baked white fish or chicken with a wedge of lemon or sprinkle of herbs.

SERVES 6

3 red or yellow (bell) peppers, halved, stalks removed, seeded and cut into thick slices
2 tablespoons olive oil
½ tablespoon sea salt, plus ½ teaspoon for the couscous
300 g (10½ oz/1½ cups) couscous
1 teaspoon madras curry powder
1 teaspoon ground cumin
75 g (2½ oz/⅔ cup) jumbo golden raisins
2 tablespoons roughly chopped flat-leaf parsley

Preheat the oven to 180°C (350°F/Gas 4).

Toss the pepper slices with the oil and sea salt in a deep roasting tin. Roast in the oven for 20 minutes, or until the peppers are soft and starting to brown. Set aside to cool and hold on to the oil the peppers roasted in.

Meanwhile put the couscous in a deep heat-proof bowl. Mix the remaining salt, curry powder, cumin and raisins through the dry couscous. Cover the couscous mixture with twice its volume of boiling water. Give the mixture a stir and cover the bowl with cling film. Set aside for 10 minutes.

Remove the cling film from the bowl and rake through the couscous with a fork to break it up. Stir the roasted peppers through the couscous and drizzle with the reserved pepper oil. Sprinkle with chopped parsley and serve.

Posh Potato Salad

This recipe is ideal for using up any leftover boiled potatoes, but in our house there are NEVER any leftovers. So, let's say this is a fab way of recycling the bacon left from a Sunday fry-up and the potatoes from a roast later that day, but to be on the safe side, just chuck an extra bag of baby spuds in your trolley when shopping for the week. LINSEY

SERVES 6

750 g (1 lb 7 oz) baby new potatoes, rinsed
   (or cold, cooked potatoes)
1 teaspoon salt
4 rashers of smoked streaky bacon
   (or cold, cooked bacon)
20 cocktail cornichons, thinly sliced
2 shallots, finely diced
200 g (7 oz) reduced-fat crème fraîche
freshly ground black pepper

Preheat the oven to 180°C (350°F/Gas 4).

If cooking the potatoes from scratch, bring a large pan of water to the boil. Add the salt and new potatoes then reduce the heat and simmer for 15 minutes.

Drain the potatoes and set aside to cool.

If cooking the bacon from scratch, arrange it on a baking sheet and cook for 15 minutes in the oven until crispy. Remove the bacon from the oven and set aside to cool on kitchen paper.

Chop the crispy bacon into thin slices (don't worry if it crumbles a bit as you chop it). Combine the cooled potatoes, bacon, cornichons, shallots and crème fraîche in a large bowl and mix well. Season with black pepper to taste.

Roasted Sweet Potato Salad

I'm obsessed with the flavour transformation of a sweet potato when it's roasted. A little good-quality extra virgin olive oil and seasoning is all they need. The seeds just add a nice bit of bite to this bright, cheery salad. LINSEY

SERVES 4

4 sweet potatoes, peeled, rinsed and cut into
  thick wedges
2 tablespoons extra virgin olive oil
2 teaspoons sea salt
150 g (5 oz/scant ⅔ cup) light natural yoghurt
2 tablespoons roughly chopped mint leaves
2 tablespoons roughly chopped flat-leaf
  parsley leaves
generous pinch of coarsely ground black pepper
3 tablespoons pumpkin seeds
1 tablespoon sunflower seeds

Preheat the oven to 180°C (350°F/Gas 4).

Toss the sweet potato wedges with the extra virgin olive oil in a deep roasting tin and sprinkle with the sea salt. Roast in the oven for 30 minutes, tossing them halfway through the cooking time to ensure they cook evenly.

Meanwhile, combine the yoghurt, herbs and seasoning in a bowl.

Remove the sweet potato wedges from the oven and set aside to cool.

To serve, arrange the sweet potato wedges on four plates, drizzle with the herbed yoghurt and sprinkle with a mixture of seeds.

Roasted Beetroot Salad

Boiling the beetroot beforehand makes removing the skins so much simpler. The flavour of roasted beetroot doesn't need to be over-complicated with too many other flavours, so I've kept this one simple, but still show-stopping. LINSEY

SERVES 6

6 large (450 g/1 lb) raw beetroot (red beet),
    cleaned, top and tail intact
2 tablespoons extra virgin olive oil
2 teaspoons fennel seeds
5 tablespoons thick Greek yoghurt
grated zest of 1 unwaxed orange
2 tablespoons roughly chopped tarragon leaves

Use a slotted spoon to lower the beetroot in a large pan of boiling water. Turn the heat down to a simmer and leave to cook for 30 minutes, or until they are soft when stabbed with a knife. Drain and leave to cool.

Preheat the oven to 180°C (350°F/Gas 4).

When cool enough to touch, peel the skins off the beetroot using your fingers (they should just slip off). Use rubber gloves if you like to stop the beetroot staining your fingers pink. Rinse the peeled beetroot under cold water, then cut them into 1-cm- (½-in-) slices.

Transfer the beetroot slices to a deep baking tin, coat with olive oil and sprinkle with the fennel seeds. Roast in the oven for 30 minutes, tossing them halfway through to ensure they cook evenly.

Remove the beetroot from the oven – it should be deeper in colour and beginning to crisp up. Leave to cool, then transfer to a serving bowl. Add the yoghurt, orange zest and tarragon, mix thoroughly and serve.

Soups

Our granny is the ultimate soup-maker and can make a broth out of any array of leftover veg you could throw at her. When we were little, we all observed the art of soup-making, standing on a stool in her kitchen as she made a daily vat of lentil soup for the customers of her sweetie shop and newsagent.

Her most popular soups were scotch broth, lentil and leek & potato to be honest, and these are the soups we still find to be most popular years later in our café. Many of our recipes are inspired by these Scottish classics, although we usually try to add a Three Sisters Bake twist.

Served with a wedge of home-baked bread, soup is truly one of life's simple pleasures. It can be frozen and reheated as a speedy meal for one, enjoyed from a flask in the middle of a campsite or shared with friends as a dinner party starter. You really don't get a more versatile food!

One of our food philosophies is that we aim to create colourful, tasty, healthy food using as many local, fresh ingredients as possible. Soup is the perfect way to tick all of these boxes, allowing our chefs to be inventive while producing a meal that is packed full of veggie goodness and without huge piles of calories. The only decadence we've slipped into this chapter is the gruyère toasties served with the French Onion Soup (page 76) – they were simply too delicious to leave out.   GILLIAN

Tomato, Rocket and Feta Soup

This is my favourite soup in the whole world! I first tried a variation of it made with goat's cheese in a lovely soup café when I was living in Dublin. Any crumbly cheese works well and really adds a great flavour and texture to this simple tomato soup. GILLIAN

SERVES 8

1.5 kg (3 lb 5 oz) ripe vine tomatoes, quartered and hard cores removed

3 red onions, quartered

2 tablespoons extra virgin olive oil

2 sprigs of thyme, leaves picked

2 large white potatoes (waxed or floury), scrubbed and cut into rough chunks

2 × 400 g (14 oz) tins of cherry tomatoes

150 g (5 oz) feta cheese, crumbled

75 g (2½ oz) rocket (arugula) leaves

3 tablespoons balsamic vinegar

3 tablespoons soft brown sugar

salt and freshly ground black pepper, to taste

Preheat the oven to 180°C (350°F/Gas 4).

Spread the tomato and onion quarters in the base of a deep roasting tin and toss with the olive oil. Sprinkle over the thyme leaves. Roast for 35 minutes, checking at regular intervals and turning the vegetables every 10 minutes or so. The onions should become nicely browned and soft and the tomato skin should shrivel up.

Remove the vegetables from the oven and transfer to a large heavy-based pan. Add the potato chunks to the pan, along with the tinned tomatoes, filling one of the empty tomato tins with water and adding this too. Bring to the boil on a high heat, then turn the heat down and simmer, uncovered, for 20 minutes, until the potatoes are soft.

Add the crumbled feta to the pan, along with the rocket leaves, balsamic vinegar and sugar. Season to taste. Leave to cool slightly.

Liquidize well, with a hand blender, until smooth. Taste and add more salt if necessary.

Lentil and Apricot Soup

I used to work as a chef in a busy lunch café in Glasgow. No matter what other exciting soups I created, lentil would always be the customer favourite. Eventually, I decided to experiment with variations on lentil so I could still be creative in my cooking whilst giving people a taste of their old classic. Lentil and apricot was the winning recipe. LINSEY

SERVES 6

1 teaspoon olive oil
25 g (1 oz) butter
1 white onion, roughly chopped into 2½-cm-
(1-in-) chunks
2 large white potatoes (floury or waxed),
scrubbed and chopped into rough chunks
4 carrots, chopped into rough chunks
2 celery sticks, tough strings removed and
roughly chopped
1 large leek, topped and tailed, chopped into
2½-cm- (1-in-) lengths and rinsed thoroughly
200 g (7 oz/¾ cup) red lentils, rinsed in a
sieve under running water, until the water
runs clear
200 g (7 oz) fresh apricots, de-stoned and
roughly chopped
1 tablespoon vegetable bouillon powder
salt and freshly ground black pepper, to taste
2 teaspoons finely chopped flat-leaf parsley,
to serve

Heat the oil and butter in a heavy-based deep pan on a medium heat. Add all the vegetables to the pan and sweat them gently for 10 minutes, stirring every couple of minutes, until soft. Add the rinsed lentils, the apricots and enough water to cover all the ingredients, turn up the heat and bring to the boil.

Once the soup is boiling, add the bouillon powder and give everything a good stir.

Now reduce the heat to a simmer and cook for 25 minutes, uncovered. Check halfway through to see if the water needs topping up at all – it should just cover the veggies.

Check the lentils are completely soft before removing from the heat. Allow to cool a little.

Liquidize well with a hand blender until smooth, then taste for seasoning and add extra salt if needed. Stir through the chopped parsley and serve.

Leek, Potato and Vanilla Soup

I am totally inclined to go from eating super-fresh, healthy dishes all summer long to craving hearty, stodgy dishes as soon as the nights draw in. This soup, made with skimmed milk, is healthy fare disguised as comfort food. It delivers a warming satisfaction without the hefty calorie hit. The addition of vanilla brings out the sweetness of the leeks and modernizes this old classic. LINSEY

SERVES 6–8

550 g (1 lb 2½ oz) leeks, topped and tailed,
  roughly chopped and rinsed thoroughly
400 g (14 oz) medium, white floury potatoes,
  scrubbed and roughly chopped
250 g (9 oz) onions, roughly chopped
1 garlic clove, crushed
1 litre (32 fl oz) skimmed milk
1 litre (32 fl oz) water
30 ml (1 fl oz) vanilla extract
25 g (1 oz) salt
freshly ground black pepper, to taste

Put the leeks, potatoes and onion in a large, heavy-based pan with the crushed garlic, milk and water. Bring to the boil on a high heat, then turn the heat down and simmer for 20 minutes, uncovered. Test the vegetables to ensure they have softened – if the potatoes are still a little hard, simmer for a further 5 minutes.

Take the pan off the heat and allow to cool a little before liquidizing the soup with a hand blender until smooth. Add the vanilla extract, seasoning and serve.

Sweet Potato, Coconut *and* Lime Soup

This is our runaway bestselling soup in the café and we are hugely proud of Linsey for inventing it. It is the type of soup that appeals no matter what the weather. It will cheer you up on a dull day, or provide comfort after the most raucous of weekends, and we love it. NICHOLA

SERVES 6

4 medium sweet potatoes, peeled and cut into 2½-cm- (1-in-) chunks
1½ white onions, cut into 2½-cm- (1-in-) chunks
4 carrots, cut into 2½-cm- (1-in-) chunks
2 × 400 ml (14 fl oz) tins of light coconut milk
grated zest of 2 limes
2 tablespoons roughly chopped coriander (cilantro), to serve
salt and freshly ground pepper

Put all the vegetables in a heavy-based deep pan and add enough cold water to almost cover them. Bring to the boil on a high heat, then turn the heat down and simmer for 20 minutes, uncovered, until the vegetables are soft.

Add the coconut milk and lime zest. Simmer for a further 5 minutes.

Remove from the heat and allow to cool a little before liquidizing until smooth with a hand blender. Season to taste. Stir through the coriander and serve.

Mushroom, Lemon and Basil Soup

I beg of you, if you think you don't like mushrooms, please do try this soup. The lemon and basil compliment one another like they were born to be a couple, transforming what could be a bit of an insipid vegetable (not my opinion, I won't hear a bad word against the humble mushroom) into something earthy and rich. The end result is a summery yet filling bowlful. LINSEY

SERVES 6

2 white onions, chopped into 2½-cm- (1-in-) chunks

2 large white potatoes, floury or waxy, scrubbed and cut into 2½-cm- (1-in-) chunks

2 celery sticks, chopped into 2½-cm- (1-in-) chunks

2 litres (3½ pints) skimmed milk

750 g (1 lb 7 oz) mushrooms (a mixture of chestnut and white mushrooms works well), cleaned and halved

grated zest of 1½ unwaxed lemons

50 g (2 oz) basil (stalks and leaves), roughly chopped

2 tablespoons crème fraîche

salt and freshly ground black pepper

Place all the vegetables in a heavy-based deep pan and add the milk. Bring to the boil on a high heat and then reduce the heat and simmer for 20 minutes, uncovered.

Add the chopped mushrooms and lemon zest to the pan. Top with enough water to nearly cover the vegetables. Simmer for a further 5 minutes.

Remove the pan from the heat and allow to cool slightly before liquidizing with a hand blender until smooth.

Now add the basil and the crème fraîche and season to taste. Reheat to serve.

Baked Potato and Crispy Bacon Soup

Soups are a fab way to use up bits and bobs of leftovers or stray veggies. This combination of homeless odds and ends is a happy marriage, the end result being a cosy bowl of comfort and joy. And it all began with a distracted chef being neglectful of her tatties baking away in the oven…

LINSEY

SERVES 6

4 large baking potatoes, scrubbed
1 tablespoon olive oil
1 tablespoon sea salt
5 rashers unsmoked back bacon
20 g (¾ oz) butter
2 medium white onions, diced
2 small garlic cloves, crushed
2 litres (3½ pints) skimmed milk (the milk gives the soup body without making it heavy)
freshly ground black pepper
a handful of flat-leaf parsley, roughly chopped, to serve

Preheat the oven to 200°C (400°F/Gas 6).

Rub the potatoes with oil, sprinkle with sea salt and bake in the oven for about 1 hour, until the potatoes are crispy and dark-skinned. The cooking time is slightly longer than you would ordinarily need to cook a potato through, but overcooking is the key to the deep-roasted flavour here. Around 20 minutes before you remove the potatoes from the oven, put the bacon rashers on a baking tray and cook in the oven until crispy. Remove the potatoes and bacon from the oven and leave to cool.

Melt the butter in a large saucepan on a medium heat. Sauté the onions in the butter for about 10 minutes or until they just begin to colour. Add the crushed garlic and milk, then top up with enough water to just cover the vegetables. Bring to the boil then turn down to simmer for 15 minutes, uncovered.

In the meantime, cut the potatoes in half and scrape out the flesh. (Scrape as close to the skin as possible – you want to get all the deep-roasted flavour from the outer layer of potato, but not the tough skin itself.) Add the potato flesh to the pan and discard the skins. Simmer for a further 5 minutes.

Chop the crispy bacon into thin slices. It will crumble a little as you chop it, but this is good.

Remove the soup from the heat, allow to cool then liquidize with a hand blender until smooth. Add the bacon and give the soup a good stir. Season with black pepper to taste. Bear in mind the soup will take on the saltiness of the bacon so taste before adding any salt. Stir through the parsley and serve.

Parsnip, Apple and Mint Soup

This is a lovely light soup which makes a perfect starter or, even better, a lunch on a sunny day. The concept of apples in soup always tends to raise an eyebrow among our more cautious customers, but after one mouthful they are convinced. NICHOLA

SERVES 8

6 medium parsnips, scrubbed and chopped
    into 1-cm- (½-in-) chunks
2 tablespoons maple or agave syrup
1 tablespoon olive oil
2 white onions, chopped into 2.5-cm- (1-in-)
    chunks
1 medium leek, topped and tailed, chopped into
    2.5-cm- (1-in-) chunks and rinsed thoroughly
2 large white floury potatoes, scrubbed and
    chopped into 2.5-cm- (1-in-) chunks
2 litres (3½ pints) skimmed milk
6 Granny Smith apples
1 teaspoon vegetable bouillon powder
salt and coarsely ground black pepper
2½ tablespoons finely chopped mint leaves,
    to serve

Preheat the oven to 160°C (320°F/Gas 2).

Place the parsnip chunks in a deep roasting tin, drizzle with the syrup and toss in the oil to coat. Roast in the oven for 25 minutes. Check every 5 minutes and give them a shake to prevent the syrup burning.

Meanwhile, put the onions, leek and potatoes in a heavy-based deep pan and cover with the milk. Bring to the boil on a high heat, then reduce the heat and simmer for 20 minutes, uncovered.

Peel, core and roughly chop the apples. Add the roasted parsnips, apples and bouillon powder to the pan. Top up with water to nearly cover the veg and simmer for a further 10 minutes.

Remove from the heat, allow to cool a little and liquidize with a hand blender until smooth. Season to taste, then scatter with the chopped mint leaves and serve.

Moroccan Aubergine Soup

This soup makes a fab flask accompaniment to a bonfire on a damp autumn night. Combining sweet-smoked paprika with smoky charred aubergine creates an amazing flavoursome soup which will warm you down to the tips of your toes. GILLIAN

SERVES 6

6 medium aubergines (eggplants), washed and dried

2 red onions, chopped into 2.5-cm- (1-in-) chunks

2 white potatoes, scrubbed and chopped into 2.5-cm- (1-in-) chunks

4 carrots, chopped into 1-cm- (½-in-) discs

2 kg (4½ lb) vine tomatoes, quartered and hard cores removed

2 × 400 g (14 oz) tins of chopped tomatoes

2 teaspoons sweet-smoked paprika

1 teaspoon ground cumin

1 teaspoon ground coriander

½ teaspoon mild curry powder

2 teaspoons salt

Preheat the oven to 200°C (400°F/Gas 6).

Arrange the whole aubergines on a baking tray and roast in the oven for 45 minutes, turning them every 15 minutes. You want to end up with a really smoky taste, which means charring the skin.

Put the chopped onions, potatoes, carrots and vine tomatoes in a heavy-based deep pan. Add the tinned tomatoes and spices, filling one of the empty tomato tins with water and adding this too. Bring to the boil on a high heat, the reduce to a simmer for 25 minutes, uncovered.

Remove the aubergines from the oven and let them cool slightly until you can handle them. Chop the tops off the aubergines, cut them in half lengthways and scoop out the flesh straight into the soup pan, allowing the juices to run into the soup too. Don't worry if a little of the charred skin gets in – it will add an extra smokiness.

Simmer for a further 5 minutes, allow to cool a little and then liquidize with a hand blender until smooth. Stir in the salt and serve.

French Onion Soup with Mini Gruyère Toasties

After years of enjoying this soup in the French Alps, I was taught to make it by a French chef at the Edinburgh School of Food and Wine. As he poured two glasses of wine, followed by two shots of brandy, into the pot, I realised why skiing always seemed easier in the afternoons.

LINSEY

SERVES 4

25 g (1 oz) salted butter
6 white onions, sliced very thinly by hand (or using a mandoline/food processor)
4 garlic cloves, sliced very thinly by hand (or using a mandoline/food processor)
350 ml (12 fl oz) red wine
850 ml (1½ pints) hot fresh beef stock (bought from your butcher or the chilled aisle at the supermarket)
30 ml (1 fl oz) brandy
5 tablespoons balsamic vinegar
salt and freshly ground black pepper, to taste

FOR THE MINI GRUYÈRE TOASTIES

2 slices of white bread
a knob of butter, for frying (and extra for spreading)
50 g (2 oz) gruyère cheese, thickly sliced
4 cocktail sticks or small wooden skewers, to serve

Heat the butter in a large heavy-based pan on a medium heat, until melted and bubbling. Add the onions and sauté for at least 20 minutes, uncovered, stirring frequently. You want them to become a deep-brown colour without burning. Add the garlic and continue to stir for a further 3 minutes.

Add the wine, hot stock, brandy and vinegar and leave to simmer for 15 minutes, uncovered.

Meanwhile, for the toasties, butter one side of each slice of bread. Place the gruyère cheese slices on the non-buttered side of one of the slices. Make a sandwich by placing the other non-buttered side on top of the cheese, leaving two buttered sides of bread facing out.

Melt a knob of butter in a frying pan on a medium-high heat. Fry the gruyère sandwich for about 5 minutes until the underside is golden brown. Flip over and fry the other side.

If the cheese has not melted, turn the heat down and continue to fry until the cheese starts to ooze out of the sandwich (but be careful not to burn the bread). Add more butter to the pan if required.

Cut the gruyère toastie into quarters and spear each quarter with a cocktail stick or wooden skewer (cocktail sticks work well if you're serving the soup in teacups; use skewers if you are serving in a soup bowl).

Remove the soup from the heat, season to taste and ladle into heatproof bowls or teacups, depending on the occasion. Place the gruyère toastie on top of the bowl or teacup and serve.

Lunch

If you were to ask any of us where our favourite place in the world is, Arran would be one of the top answers. Arran is an island off the west coast of Scotland where we spent many happy summers as children. The island is sometimes called 'Scotland in miniature' due to its mountains, valleys, beaches and generally spectacular scenery.

Half the fun of going to Arran on holiday was that it had to be accessed by ferry, a journey that we found almost as exciting as the holiday itself. We spent our days pottering around in rock pools, visiting the island's candy floss shop and building sandcastle villages.

The main activity of the day, however, would be the ceremonial preparation and consumption of our lunch picnic. The process of acquiring food for the picnic began almost as soon as breakfast ended. We would all walk to the tiny local baker's shop to buy rolls, followed by a visit to the village butcher for some of his homemade corned beef and the dairy to buy cheese. Deciding what combination of cheese, meats and condiments to put in each roll was so drawn out that it would be nearly lunchtime by the time the picnic bag was finally packed.

Occasionally we would venture off in the car to one of the island's other villages in search of a new picnic spot, but most often we would decamp to the beach to enjoy our carefully crafted rolls, crisps and juice before spending the rest of the afternoon running in and out of the water.

We still visit Arran as often as we can, but it can be difficult to fit in with the various commitments of running a café. Now that Gillian and I have families of our own, we will be keeping up the tradition of picnicking on the beach as soon as our wee ones are old enough to walk to the baker's shop!

NICHOLA

Quinoa and Butternut Squash Cakes

These are really good served with a big salad, homemade mayo and a little lime wedge to squeeze over the top.

SERVES 4 (2 PER PERSON)

200 g (7 oz/1 cup) quinoa, rinsed until the
    water runs clear
1 kg (2 lb 3 oz) butternut squash (pumpkin),
    peeled, halved, seeds removed and cut into
    5-cm- (2-in-) chunks
3 teaspoons extra virgin olive oil
1 teaspoon dried chilli (chile) flakes
20 g (¾ oz) unsalted butter
2 small shallots, finely diced
1 red (bell) pepper, halved, stalk removed,
    seeded and finely diced
2 garlic cloves, crushed
2 tablespoons roughly chopped tarragon leaves
1 teaspoon salt
½ teaspoon coarsely ground black pepper
150 g (5 oz) ground almonds
75 g (2½ oz/⅚ cup) flaked almonds
crème fraîche or Homemade Mayo (page 131),
    to serve
1 lime, cut into wedges, to serve

Preheat the oven to 190°C (375°F/Gas 5).

Bring 400 ml (14 fl oz) lightly salted water to
the boil in a medium-sized saucepan. Add the
quinoa, lower the heat and simmer for 15–20
minutes, until the water is absorbed and the
quinoa is tender but with still a little bite to it.
Set aside to cool.

Place the butternut squash chunks in a deep
roasting tin, coat with 2 teaspoons of the oil

and sprinkle with the dried chilli flakes. Roast
in the oven for 30 minutes, or until the squash
is tender, tossing the chunks halfway through
the cooking time.

Meanwhile, melt half the butter in a frying pan
on a medium heat and sauté the shallots until
soft and golden. Add the red pepper and sauté
for a further 5 minutes, until soft. Add the
garlic and cook for a minute, then remove the
pan from the heat and leave to cool.

Remove the butternut squash from the oven.
Mash together while it is still hot and leave
to cool.

In a large bowl, combine the cooked quinoa,
mashed squash, onion mixture, tarragon, salt,
pepper and ground almonds. Divide and shape
the mixture into 8 patties.

Spread the flaked almonds on a clean surface.
Roll the edges of the quinoa cakes in the flaked
almonds to coat.

Heat the remaining oil and butter in a large,
heavy-based frying pan on a medium-high
heat. Add the cakes (4 at a time if possible), and
fry for 4–5 minutes on each side until they are
thoroughly heated through and golden brown
on the outside. Turn each cake onto its edge in
the pan, rolling it to toast all the almond flakes.

Serve warm with a dollop of crème fraîche or
mayo and a wedge of lime.

Beetroot Quiche

*There are times when shop-bought pastry is more than adequate.
However, it is so worth spending the time making homemade pastry for
this quiche. For twenty minutes' work, you are rewarded with a buttery,
light, melting pastry shell to fill with any of your favourite flavours.*

SERVES 8

EQUIPMENT:
25 cm (10 in) loose-bottomed, fluted flan tin
baking beans

FOR THE PASTRY
250 g (9 oz/2 cups) plain (all-purpose) flour,
   plus extra for kneading and rolling
pinch of salt
150 g (5 oz) chilled unsalted butter, cubed
1 large egg, beaten

FOR THE FILLING
40 g (1½ oz) rocket (arugula) leaves
15 teaspoons Beetroot and Walnut Pâté
   (page 96)
8 large eggs
400 ml (14 fl oz) double (heavy) cream
salt and freshly ground black pepper

For the pastry, place the flour, salt and butter
in a food processor and whizz briefly until
the mixture resembles coarse breadcrumbs.
Add the egg and pulse until the mixture just
comes together.

Tip the dough out onto a lightly floured clean
surface and knead briefly. Shape the dough
into a ball, flatten slightly, then wrap in cling
film and chill in the fridge for 30 minutes.
The pastry can be kept in the fridge like this
for up to three days.

When you are ready to make the quiche
preheat the oven to 180°C (350°F/Gas 4).

Remove the pastry from the fridge and let
it warm up a little (for around 20 minutes).
Roll out the pastry on a lightly floured surface.
It should be no thicker than 3 mm and around
30 cm (12 in) in diameter. Line the flan tin.
Cover with greaseproof (wax) paper and fill
with baking beans. 'Blind' bake the pastry case
for 20–25 minutes, until golden brown.
Remove from the oven and lift out the paper
and beans.

Sprinkle the pastry case with the rocket. Dot
evenly spaced teaspoons of the beetroot and
walnut pâté on top.

Beat the eggs and cream together in a bowl,
season, and gently pour over the rocket and
beetroot filling.

Carefully transfer the filled quiche to the oven
and cook for 25 minutes until the centre is set
(no longer wobbly).

Allow to cool a little before removing from the
tin to serve.

VARIATION
*For an alternative filling try a couple of handfuls
of spinach, 75 g (2 oz) toasted pine nuts (pine
kernels) and 12 slices of brie instead of the rocket
and the Beetroot and Walnut Pâté.*

Scottish Oatcakes

Our granny can't get her head around why oatcakes are available in the supermarket. In her day it was a given that you made staples like this from scratch, especially if it saved you money. Saving the leftover fat when you cook bacon or sausages is typical Scottish habit, and it adds flavour. These oatcakes are lovely with pâté, hummus or just cheese and chutney.

MAKES 15–20 OATCAKES

150 g (5 oz/1½ cups) pinhead oatmeal, plus extra for kneading and rolling
½ teaspoon bicarbonate of soda (baking soda)
½ teaspoon salt
3 teaspoons melted fat (leftover from cooking bacon or sausages) or melted butter, plus extra for greasing

Preheat the oven to 180°C (350°F/Gas 4).

Grease 2 baking trays with a little butter or leftover fat.

Place the oatmeal, bicarbonate of soda and salt in a large bowl and mix together. Add the melted fat or butter and a tablespoon of boiling water and stir thoroughly to combine and create an oaty dough.

Turn the dough out onto a clean work surface sprinkled with a little oatmeal and knead briefly until it becomes less sticky and easier to manage. You may need to sprinkle a little more oatmeal over the dough to achieve this.

Divide the dough into two pieces to prevent it from cracking and, working with one at a time, flatten each piece with your palm or a rolling pin, turning it often to ensure it doesn't stick to the surface. Roll out each piece until it is ½ cm (¼ in) thick, then, using a round cutter or sharp knife, cut the dough into circles, squares or triangles.

Place the oatcakes on the greased baking sheets and bake for 30–35 minutes until they are nicely browned around the edges.

Transfer to a wire rack to cool.

Sweet Potato Fish Cakes

*Using sweet potato and polenta in these fish cakes in place of regular
potato makes them a lighter dish, perfect for lunchtime.* LINSEY

SERVES 4 (2 PER PERSON)

2 medium sweet potatoes
450 g (1 lb) skinless salmon fillets, each fillet
    cut into four pieces
4 teaspoons olive oil
1 teaspoon ground cumin
2 teaspoons sea salt
15 g (½ oz) unsalted butter
3 spring onions (scallions), sliced
2 cm (1 in) piece of fresh ginger, grated
2 garlic cloves, crushed
grated zest of 2 limes
3 tablespoons roughly chopped coriander
    (cilantro)
1 large egg, beaten
100 g (3½ oz/⅔ cup) fine polenta

Preheat the oven to 200°C (400°F/Gas 6).

Prick the sweet potatoes with a fork, place
them on a baking tray and roast in the oven
for 40 minutes, until the potatoes are very soft
when pierced with a knife. Set aside to cool a
little and turn the oven temperature down to
170°C (335°F/Gas 3).

Arrange the pieces of salmon in a deep roasting
tin and coat with half of the oil. Sprinkle with
the cumin and sea salt, and bake in the oven for
10 minutes.

Remove the salmon from the oven, transfer to
a bowl and flake the flesh with a fork. Set aside
to cool.

Melt the butter in a frying pan on a medium
heat and sauté the spring onions, stirring for
5 minutes until soft and golden. Add the ginger,
garlic and lime zest and fry for one more
minute. Remove from the heat and leave to
cool slightly.

Slice open the sweet potatoes and scoop out
the flesh, transferring it to a large bowl
(discarding the skin). Add the salmon, spring
onion mixture and coriander, and mix gently
so as not to break up the salmon further.

Shape the mixture into 8 medium-sized
patties. Place the egg and polenta seperately
in 2 shallow dishes. Dip each fish cake into the
beaten egg, then coat in the polenta.

Heat the remaining oil in a large frying pan on
a medium heat. Fry 2 fish cakes at a time for
5 minutes on each side until golden and crisp.
Serve warm.

Black Pudding and Apple Sausage Rolls

Black pudding: such a crowd splitter. In our eyes this Scottish delicacy can do no wrong. It originated on the Isle of Stornoway and true Stornoway black pudding remains the best. It has a slight spice to it, which the sweetness of the apple cuts right through. LINSEY

MAKES 6 LARGE SAUSAGE ROLLS

2 small Granny Smith apples, peeled, cored and quartered
30 g (1 oz) unsalted butter
450 g (1 lb) good-quality (preferably Stornoway) black pudding, cut into 1-cm- (½-in-) cubes
400 g (14 oz) pack of ready-rolled, all-butter puff pastry
plain (all-purpose) flour, for dusting
1 large egg, beaten
sesame seeds, for sprinkling (optional)

Preheat the oven to 200°C (400°F/Gas 6).

Cut the apple into small ½-cm- (¼-in-) cubes.

Melt the butter in a frying pan on a medium heat. Add the apple cubes and gently sauté for about 10 minutes, stirring frequently, until they are golden brown. Remove the pan from the heat, transfer the apples to a bowl and set aside.

Add the black pudding cubes to the frying pan and return to a medium heat (the fat from the black pudding is sufficient for it to cook in, so there's no need for extra). As the black pudding cooks, use a wooden spoon to break it up thoroughly. Fry for 5 minutes, by which time it will be deep in colour and start to brown. Remove from the heat and set aside to cool a little before adding the cooked apple and stirring together.

Lay the puff pastry on a clean, lightly floured surface. Using your hands, place the black pudding and apple mixture in a long mound along the centre of the length of the pastry. Squash it into an even, thick sausage shape.

Lift up the edge of the pastry closest to you and roll it over the top of the black pudding and apple mixture to enclose it. Brush the edges with egg wash to seal the join and trim off and discard any excess pastry. Cut into 6 large sausage rolls before placing on a well-floured baking sheet. Brush the tops with the remaining beaten egg.

Sprinkle with sesame seeds (if using) and bake in the oven for 15–20 minutes until the pastry is puffed and golden brown.

Smoked Haddock, Spring Onion and Pea Tortilla

We have an increasing number of customers with gluten intolerances, so this was created for them as an alternative to quiche. Any number of fillings can be used here, but the smoked haddock combined with delicate spring onion and potato makes for a rich, filling meal in a slice.

SERVES 8

3 teaspoons olive oil
1 white onion, finely diced
1 garlic clove, crushed
3 boiled, unpeeled floury potatoes,
    roughly diced
300 g (10½ oz) smoked haddock (about 2
    medium fillets), cut into 1-cm- (½-in-) cubes
50 g (2 oz) frozen peas, rinsed
20 g (¾ oz) bunch of fresh dill, finely chopped
10 large eggs
100 ml (3½ fl oz) double (heavy) cream
salt and freshly ground black pepper
2 spring onions (scallions), finely sliced

Preheat the oven to 160°C (320°F/Gas 2).

Heat 2 teaspoons of the oil in a frying pan on a medium heat then add the onion and garlic and cook until soft. Add the potatoes, haddock, peas and dill. Cook for 5 minutes, stirring occasionally, ensuring the haddock remains intact. Leave to cool.

Whisk the eggs and cream together in a large bowl and season with salt and pepper. Add the cooled fish mixture to the eggs and cream, stirring gently to avoid breaking up the haddock too much.

In a wide, ovenproof, non-stick frying pan heat the remaining oil, pour in the egg and fish mixture, then scatter over the sliced spring onions. Cook on a low heat for 5 minutes, then transfer to the oven for 20 minutes, or until the eggs are just cooked.

Allow to cool for 15 minutes before removing from the pan. Then slice and serve warm.

Salmon Sandwich with Beetroot and Walnut Paté

This is a spin on a classic smoked salmon on brown bread sandwich. If you don't have the time (or inclination!) to bake your own bread, a good-quality brown loaf will work well. If you can get your hands on a brown Irish soda loaf, even better. The beetroot and walnut pâté gives the sandwich a subtle and interesting depth of flavour. NICHOLA

MAKES 3 OPEN SANDWICHES

FOR THE BEETROOT AND WALNUT PÂTÉ
6 raw beetroot (red beet) (approx. 450 g/1 lb), cleaned, top and tail intact
200 g (7 oz/2 cups) walnut halves
400 g (14 oz/1²⁄₃ cups) reduced-fat cream cheese
25 g (1 oz) fresh dill
4 tablespoons balsamic vinegar
50 g (2 oz/½ cup) dried breadcrumbs

6 large slices of Irish Soda Bread (page 122)
6 generous slices of good-quality smoked salmon
wedge of lemon, to serve
springs of dill, to garnish

Boil the whole beetroot for an hour, skin on. When cool enough to touch, use your fingertips to peel the skins off the beetroot. Wear rubber gloves if you like, to stop the beetroot staining your fingers pink.

Preheat the oven to 180°C (350°F/Gas 4).

Spread the walnuts on a baking tray for 5–10 minutes in the oven until golden and fragrant. Alternatively, you can toast them in a dry frying pan on a medium-high heat.

Roughly chop the cooked, cooled beetroot and place in the bowl of a food processor with the toasted walnuts, cream cheese, most of the dill (set aside some for garnishing) and the balsamic vinegar. Pulse, slowly adding the breadcrumbs, until the pâté reaches the same consistency as hummus, holding its shape when scooped up with a spoon.

To assemble the sandwiches spread each slice of soda bread with 2 tablespoons of the beetroot pâté. Arrange the smoked salmon on top of the pâté to create an open sandwich. Squeeze lemon juice over the top and serve garnished with dill.

Halloumi, Olive Tapenade and Spinach Flatbreads

I love cheese more than any food in the whole world. I can clearly remember the day I encountered halloumi for the first time, barbecued on skewers by an Australian friend. I was immediately hooked on its chewy, squeaky texture. Since then, much time has been spent experimenting with a variety of halloumi-based meals and sandwiches. This is one of my favourites. GILLIAN

SERVES 2

FOR THE TAPENADE
200 g (7 oz/1½ cups) pitted black olives
1 garlic clove
grated zest and juice of ½ unwaxed lemon
1 tablespoon capers, rinsed and drained
4 anchovy fillets (we use the little tins of
   anchovies in oil)
3 tablespoons extra virgin olive oil
pinch of coarsely ground black pepper
1 tablespoon chopped flat-leaf parsley

1 teaspoon olive oil
250 g (9 oz) halloumi cheese, cut into
   6 slices
2 Flatbreads (page 118)
50 g (2 oz) baby spinach leaves, washed
   thoroughly and drained
1 lemon cut into wedges, to serve

Put all the tapenade ingredients into a food processor and whizz for 10–20 seconds (not for too long: you want the tapenade to have a rough texture).

Heat a non-stick griddle pan on a high heat then add the oil. Cook the halloumi slices in the hot pan for 3 minutes on each side until golden brown.

Slice the flatbreads open at one side to make pockets. Spread 2 tablespoons of tapenade in each, topped with 3 griddled halloumi slices and baby spinach leaves.

Squeeze a wedge of lemon over each flatbread and serve immediately.

Chicken and Mango Salad with Raita

*Try to get your hands on a really ripe, sweet mango for this recipe.
This would also be beautiful dressed with our Elderflower Dressing
(page 105), with the raita on the side.*

SERVES 2

2 skinless chicken breasts (approx. 250 g/9 oz
   in total), cubed
2 tablespoons olive oil
½ teaspoon ground coriander
½ teaspoon smoked paprika
½ teaspoon ground cumin
1 large ripe mango, peeled, de-stoned and cut
   into strips
100 g (3½ oz) baby leaf salad
2 Flatbreads (page 118), to serve

FOR THE RAITA
⅓ cucumber, cut into small dice
2 tablespoons roughly chopped fresh
   mint leaves
150 g (5 oz) small pot of natural yoghurt
salt and freshly ground black pepper

Place the chicken in a bowl with the olive oil
and spices. Cover and refrigerate for an hour.

Meanwhile make the raita. Mix all the ingredients in a bowl. Season and chill until ready
to use.

Heat a wok or a frying pan on a medium heat.
Fry the marinated chicken in the oil from the
bowl for 5–10 minutes, until it is cooked
through.

Divide the salad leaves between 2 shallow
bowls. Top with the chicken, mango slices
and a spoonful of raita. Serve with flatbreads.

Baby Purées

I was slightly concerned throughout my pregnancy that running a business with a new baby might turn into a major disaster, but Rosie – born nine months after the café opened – immediately became part of the Three Sisters Bake family. I also discovered that having a kitchen full of vegetables at my disposal gave me plenty of opportunities to experiment with baby purées! GILLIAN

Cheesy Sweet Potato Purée

When I started weaning Rosie everyone told me to start with carrots or sweet potato as all babies love these. Not true! Rosie would spit out my carefully prepared purées and force me to resort to (expensive!) pouches of shop-bought baby purée. Until I discovered that, like her mum, she absolutely loves cheese! I started adding cheese to her carrots and sweet potatoes and she couldn't eat them quickly enough. GILLIAN

MAKES 12–14 BABY PORTIONS

1 large sweet potato, peeled and cubed
2 large carrots, peeled and thickly sliced
200 g (7 oz) cauliflower, roughly chopped
100 g (3½ oz) Cheddar cheese

Bring a large pan of water to the boil then add the sweet potato and carrots. Simmer for 15 minutes, then add the cauliflower. Continue cooking at a gentle simmer for 10 minutes until the vegetables are tender, then take the pan off the heat.

Save 200 ml (7 fl oz) of the vegetable cooking water and drain away the rest. Return the saved water to the pan with the vegetables and blend with a hand blender until very smooth (for a baby aged 6–7 months), or mash by hand for an older baby. Grate the cheese over the purée and stir through.

Freeze any leftover purée in ice-cube trays, then pop the ice cubes out into a freezer bag, and label.

Pear and Parsnip Purée

I adapted this purée from one of our winter soup recipes after struggling to get my little fussy eater to eat parsnips. Cooking the pears in a little juice ensures they do not lose their sweetness during cooking and convinced Rosie to eat parsnips by the bucket! GILLIAN

MAKES 12–14 BABY PORTIONS

4 parsnips, peeled and roughly chopped
4 pears, peeled, cored and roughly chopped
150 ml (5 fl oz) pear juice or apple juice
    (fresh, not from concentrate)

Bring a large pan of water to the boil then add the chopped parsnips, turn down the heat and simmer for 25 minutes.

Meanwhile, place the chopped pears in a separate pan, pour in the pear or apple juice and top up with enough boiling water to just about cover the pears. Place the pan on a low-medium heat, bring to a simmer and cook, stirring, for 15 minutes.

Drain the cooked parsnips then return them to their pan, adding the cooked pears in their cooking water/juice. Blend with a hand blender until very smooth (for a baby aged 6–7 months) or mash by hand for an older baby.

Salad Dressings

There is no need for a cocktail of complicated ingredients to dress good-quality vegetables. We try to keep it pretty simple and use a select few flavours to bring out the best in our salads. It makes sense to use other natural ingredients to compliment our raw veg – we are constantly looking for ways to use fruits and wild herbs to lift our lovely salads.

Charred Orange and Olive Oil Dressing

This dressing originated during barbeque season a couple of years ago. When the weather is nice enough to drag the barbeque out of hiding, we really make the most of the moment and experiment with anything and everything on it. Charring the oranges gives this dressing it's depth, with a slight smokiness.

MAKES 120 ML (4 FL OZ)

1 orange
5 tablespoons extra virgin olive oil
1 tablespoon agave or maple syrup
1 tablespoon white balsamic vinegar
a small pinch of coarsely ground black pepper

If you have the barbecue fired up, use it to char the orange. If not, a griddle pan will do the job: cut the orange in half across the middle. Brush the surface with a little oil, before placing the halves, face down, on the barbecue or griddle pan. Leave for around 10 minutes, until the orange begins to soften and turn dark brown. Remove from the heat and set aside to cool.

When cool enough to handle, juice the orange into a bowl, allowing some charred bits to fall through. Thoroughly whisk in the remaining ingredients.

Elderflower Dressing

This is a really delicate dressing and, with the elderflower being such a subtle taste, it is best teamed with white fish or chicken. We have an elderflower patch just down the path from the café, so make our own elderflower vinegar in the summer, but it is available from most delis or large supermarkets.

MAKES 100 ML (3½ FL OZ)

2 teaspoons elderflower cordial
4 teaspoons elderflower vinegar
4 tablespoons extra virgin olive oil
¼ teaspoon French Dijon mustard
a small pinch of salt
a small pinch of white pepper

Place all the ingredients in a bowl and whisk thoroughly.

House Dressing

We dress all of our leafy side salads with our staple Three Sisters Bake house dressing and are frequently asked for the recipe. Its slightly sweet finish complements most salads or vegetables but we also use it to add a savoury edge to fruity dishes.

MAKES 350 ML (12 FL OZ)

125 ml (4 fl oz/½ cup) vegetable oil
125 ml (4 fl oz/½ cup) raspberry vinegar
115 g (3⅔ oz/½ cup) caster (superfine) sugar
1 tablespoon clear honey
a pinch of salt
a pinch of coarsely ground black pepper

Place all the ingredients in a bowl and whisk thoroughly.

Iced Tea

When we moved to Quarriers Village, one of the very first people to visit us was our neighbour, Anita, from Jenier Teas, who just happened to be a world-class tea supplier! We were delighted to discover such a gem on our doorstep and now stock a full range of her delicious teas in our café and use one called 'Duchess Earl Grey' in this summery iced tea.

GILLIAN

SERVES 8

8 heaped teaspoons good-quality loose-leaf Earl Grey tea
1.2 litres (2 pints) boiling water
juice of 2 lemons
8 teaspoons caster (superfine) sugar (more or less to taste)
ice cubes, to serve
fresh lemon slices, to serve

Place the tea leaves in a large teapot or heat-proof jug, add boiling water and leave to infuse for around 4 minutes (longer if you enjoy a strong brew!).

Pour the mixture through a fine sieve into another heatproof jug to extract the leaves. Discard the leaves, add the lemon juice, then slowly stir in the sugar, stopping regularly to taste. Add sugar until your preferred level of sweetness has been achieved.

Leave to cool and then chill for 2 hours.

Serve with plenty of ice cubes and a lemon slice in each glass or teacup.

Bread

Before I discovered cooking, my first real passion was skiing. I spent two winter seasons working in chalets in the French resort of Val d'Isere. I worked every morning and evening, cooking breakfast and dinner for the chalet's guests, and spent each day racing across the slopes, always trying to fit in one more run before it was time to head back to the village.

My first job of the day was collecting baguettes and flutes for the chalet guests from the local boulangerie at 6.30AM. The delicious smell of baking bread permeated the entire village but was particularly intoxicating in the bakery itself. I would watch in fascination as the daily process of preparing and baking croissants, pain au chocolat, tarts and breads of all shapes and sizes took place before most of the village was even awake.

Before we opened the café we were determined that we would bake our own breads on site. It is something that very few cafés in Scotland do due to the equipment and manpower required, but we knew we needed to set high standards in order to stand out. It took six months of hard work, looking for an experienced baker and sourcing suitable equipment but finally we got there. No matter what stresses have occurred the day before, arriving at the café every morning to the smell of freshly baked focaccia still makes me smile and provides a daily reminder of why we chose to run a café.

LINSEY

Sea Salt and Oregano Focaccia

We love focaccia because it is EASY, something which cannot be said about many bread recipes! Sea salt and oregano focaccia is our staple sandwich bread at the café, as it lends itself to just about any filling. It also tastes great as a light and fluffy dipping bread for hummus or olive oil. NICHOLA

MAKES 1 LOAF

EQUIPMENT:
23 × 33 cm (9 × 13 in) roasting tin

900g (2 lbs/7½ cups) strong white bread flour, plus extra for dusting
2 teaspoons salt
2 × 7 g (½ oz) sachets instant yeast
70 ml (2½ fl oz) olive oil, plus extra for greasing and drizzling
3 teaspoons sea salt
a handful of fresh oregano
balsamic vinegar, for dipping

Grease the roasting tin with olive oil.

Place the flour, salt and yeast into a large bowl, or the bowl of a freestanding mixer fitted with a dough hook. Make a well in the centre then pour in 600 ml (1 pint) of tepid water and the olive oil. Knead the dough by hand or machine for 10 minutes. To knead by hand, first bring the dough together in the bowl, then turn it out onto a floured surface and continue to knead. The dough should look smooth and glossy and feel stretchy when pulled.

Place the dough in the roasting tin, shape into a rough rectangle, then cover the tin with oiled cling film. Leave to rise in a warm place until doubled in size – this will take about 1½ hours.

Preheat the oven to 180°C (350°F/Gas 4).

Remove the cling film and pull the dough from the middle into the corners of the tin. Sprinkle with sea salt and fresh oregano. Press your fingers into the dough to create the focaccia dimples and drizzle with olive oil.

Place a roasting tin with a few ice cubes in the bottom of the oven to create steam – it enhances this bread, and keeps it from going too dry as it bakes. Bake the focaccia in the oven for 16–18 minutes.

Serve hot or cold, with extra virgin olive oil and balsamic vinegar for dipping.

VARIATION
Instead of sea salt and oregano, try scattering sautéed red onions, black olives or sun-dried tomatoes over the dough just before baking for a totally different flavour.

Rye and Raisin Bread

*This bread tastes amazing toasted for breakfast and spread with butter.
It also works well with a savoury lunch, such as a Ploughman's Platter
(pages 134–135), or simply with a slab of good-quality pâté and
Homemade Red Onion Marmalade (page 34).* GILLIAN

MAKES 1 LOAF

200 g (7 oz/1²/₃ cups) strong white bread flour,
  plus extra for dusting
50 g (2 oz/½ cup) dark rye flour
5 g (¹/₆ oz) instant yeast
a pinch of salt
100 g (3½ oz/generous ¾ cup) raisins
olive oil, for greasing

Place the flours, yeast and salt into a large mixing bowl, or the bowl of a freestanding mixer fitted with a dough hook. Mix briefly, then add 175 ml (6 fl oz) tepid water and mix to form a sticky dough.

Knead the dough by hand or machine for 10 minutes, adding the raisins in the final minute of kneading. To knead by hand, first bring the dough together in the bowl, then turn it out onto a floured surface and continue to knead. The dough should feel soft and springy to the touch.

Place the dough in a lightly greased bowl. Cover with a clean, damp tea towel and leave to prove in a warm place for 1 hour or until doubled in size.

Turn out the dough onto a lightly floured surface and knead for a couple of minutes, then shape into a ball.

Place the loaf on a greased baking sheet, and cut a deep 'X' into the top (about 1 cm/½ in deep), using a very sharp knife. Cover with a well-floured tea towel and leave to rise in a warm, draught-free place for 45 minutes or until doubled in size.

Preheat the oven to 180°C (350°F/Gas 4).

Remove the tea towel and bake in the oven for 45 minutes or until the bread sounds hollow when the base is tapped. Remove from the oven and place to cool on a wire rack.

Sourdough Starter

Making a sourdough starter takes a bit of dedication but we promise it's worth the effort. Once you have built up a healthy culture you can maintain it for years (ours is three years old!). We feed ours every day but if you only plan to use your starter sporadically, we recommend keeping it the fridge and feeding it once a week. GILLIAN

strong white bread flour
tepid water

Mix 50 g (2 oz/scant ½ cup) of flour and 50 ml (2 fl oz) of tepid water in a sealable plastic container or jar. Stir it well, cover with a lid and leave at room temperature for 24 hours.

On the second day, add the same amount of fresh flour and water, stir again, cover and leave at room temperature for another 24 hours.

Repeat on the third day. If all goes well, that might be enough to create an active starter, which will be 'fizzing' and should be covered with bubbles. Your starter may, however, take a few more days to reach this stage. If it is not 'fizzing' after three days, remove about half of it, and add another 75 g (2½ oz/scant ⅔ cup)

strong white bread flour and 75 ml (3 fl oz) tepid water. It may take up to 7 or 8 days of repeating this process for the yeasts and lactic bacteria to settle and combine.

It should be ready to use after 5 days. To feed the starter, remove half of the mixture from the container (either use it in a recipe or discard it) and refresh it with 75 g (2½ oz/scant ⅔ cup) strong white bread flour and 75 ml (3 fl oz) tepid water.

You should aim to feed your starter with equal parts water and flour every day or two if kept at room temperature, or once a week if chilled. If you are storing it in the fridge, revive the mixture by taking it out of the fridge a few days before you intend to use it and start feeding it daily.

Sourdough Bread

We won't deny that this is a more complex bread to put together than some of the others in this chapter. Trust us though that the time spent kneading, folding and waiting for the bread to rise is completely worth it. The time you put in time will pay off – the difference in depth of flavour and the texture of this sourdough compared to a standard white loaf is immense. LINSEY

MAKES 2 LOAVES

450 g (1 lb/3½ cups) strong white bread flour,
    plus extra for dusting
175 g (6 oz) Sourdough Starter (opposite)
10 g (⅓ oz) salt
oil, for greasing

Place the flour in a large bowl. In a separate bowl combine 240 ml (8 fl oz) tepid water and the starter, then add this to the flour. Mix to form a sticky dough.

Bring together in the bowl first and then turn the dough out onto a floured surface to knead. Alternatively, knead the dough in the bowl of a freestanding mixer fitted with a dough hook, adding the salt towards the end of the kneading. After about 10 minutes of kneading the dough should be smooth and elastic.

Place the dough in a large oiled bowl, cover with a clean, damp tea towel and leave it to prove in a warm place for 1 hour. (Sourdough does not double in size like other doughs because there is no yeast in the mixture.)

Turn out the dough onto a clean, lightly oiled surface. Carefully stretch it out then fold it back into the middle one side at a time. Spin 90 degrees and repeat the stretching and folding motion.

Put the dough back in the bowl to rest. After another hour stretch and fold again then place the dough back in the bowl for 30 minutes.

Tip the dough onto an oiled surface. Divide it into two equal pieces and shape each one into a loaf and place seam-side up in a bowl lined with a heavily floured cloth. Cover with lightly-oiled cling film and leave to prove for 2 hours in a warm spot.

Preheat the oven to 220°C (425°F/Gas 7).

Put a few ice cubes or cold water into a baking tin and place in the bottom of the oven to create steam.

Turn out the loaves onto a baking tray. Using a thin sharp knife score a line along the top of the loaves. Bake in the oven for 35 minutes or until a golden crust has formed and the loaves sound hollow when tapped on the base. Place on a wire rack to cool.

Flatbread

It takes a brave and keen cook to launch themselves into the art of bread-making, however this simple recipe should put any apprehensions to bed. It's pretty quick, doesn't require expensive equipment and there's no tinkering with yeast. We love to serve flatbreads with our Halloumi and Olive Tapenade and Chicken and Mango Salad with Raita (pages 98–99). LINSEY

MAKES 10 FLATBREADS

200 g (7 oz/ 1 ⅔ cups) white self-raising flour, plus a little extra for dusting
200 g (7 oz/1½ cups) wholemeal self-raising flour
1 tablespoon sea salt
1 tablespoon baking powder
400 g (14 oz/3 cups) natural yoghurt

Place all the ingredients in the bowl of a food processor and pulse until you have a soft dough. Alternatively, combine the ingredients by hand in a large bowl.

Turn out the dough onto a lightly floured surface and knead for a couple of minutes. Divide the dough into 10 equal-sized balls. Lightly dust a rolling pin and roll each ball of dough out until it is 3–4 mm (¼ in) thick. Don't worry if they are not perfectly circular – they look better a little haphazard.

Once you have rolled out all the flatbreads, place a non-stick griddle pan on a high heat and give it 5 minutes to get nice and hot. Cook the flatbreads for 2 minutes on each side, until each has puffed up a little and has charred lines. Serve warm.

Tattie Scones

*Potato scones, or 'tattie' scones, are a staple of any Scottish fry-up.
They taste absolutely delicious fried in a bit of oil but can be made
into a relatively healthy breakfast accompaniment by toasting
them under the grill.* NICHOLA

MAKES 10–12

500 g (1 lb 2 oz) floury potatoes, peeled and cut
    into quarters
100 g (3½ oz/scant cup) plain (all-purpose)
    flour, sifted, plus extra for dusting
15 g (½ oz) salted butter, softened
generous pinch of salt
⅓ teaspoon baking powder
1 teaspoon olive oil

Cook the potatoes in a large pan of salted
boiling water for 15 minutes, until soft. Drain,
then tip into a large bowl and leave them to
cool for 10 minutes.

Add the flour, butter, salt and baking powder
to the potatoes and then mash everything
together. Don't worry about getting the mix
completely smooth.

Use your hands to bring the mixture together
and transfer it to a clean, floured work surface.
Using a floured rolling pin, roll out the potato
mixture to an even 2-cm- (¾-in-) thick disc.

We use a 12 cm (4½ in) round cutter, but trad-
itionally tattie scones are cut into triangles
– cut them into whichever shape you prefer.

Heat the olive oil in a shallow frying pan on
a medium heat. Fry the potato scones for
2 minutes on each side until golden brown and
slightly puffy. Be careful when turning them as
they are a little more fragile than a shop-
bought version.

American-style Cornbread Muffins

*We serve pulled pork sliders on these great little cornbread muffins
as part of our Soul BBQ evening menu – they are delicious! The slightly
sweet bread complements a savoury filling perfectly.* LINSEY

MAKES 10 MUFFINS

EQUIPMENT:
12-hole muffin tray

175 g (6 oz/1½ cup) plain (all-purpose) flour
100 g (3½ oz/ ⅔ cup) polenta
½ teaspoon salt
2 teaspoons baking powder
50 g (2 oz/scant ¼ cup) caster (superfine) sugar
240 ml (8½ fl oz) whole (full-cream) milk
1 large egg at room temperature
50 g (2 oz) unsalted butter, melted, plus extra
   for greasing
100 g (3½ oz/½ cup) sweetcorn kernels
   (tinned or fresh)

Preheat the oven to 180°C (350°F/Gas 4).

Grease the muffin tray with a little melted
butter or spray oil.

Place all the ingredients (except the sweetcorn)
in a large bowl and mix together. Add the sweetcorn and mix briefly until well combined.

Pour the mixture into the muffin tray and bake
in the oven for 15 minutes, until they spring
back to shape when lightly touched. Turn out
and allow to cool on a wire rack.

Irish Soda Bread

*I spent four years living in Dublin and became thoroughly addicted
to soda bread (or 'brown bread' as it is called in Ireland). Irish soda
bread is quite a dense loaf which makes it a versatile accompaniment
to breakfast, lunch or dinner. It is also eaten in Ireland for elevenses
(the best meal of the day) slathered in butter and jam.* GILLIAN

MAKES 1 LOAF

EQUIPMENT:
23 cm (9 in) baking tin

225 g (8 oz/1½ cups) strong wholemeal flour
225 g (8 oz/1¾ cups) strong white (all-purpose)
   flour, plus extra for dusting
1 teaspoon salt
1 teaspoon bicarbonate of soda (baking soda)
25 g (1 oz) chilled unsalted butter, cubed
1 large egg
200 ml (7 fl oz) whole (full-cream) milk
200 g (7 oz/generous ¾ cup) natural yoghurt

Preheat the oven to 180°C (350°F/Gas 4). Line
the baking tin with greaseproof (wax) paper.

Sift the flours, salt and bicarbonate of soda
into a large bowl. Add the butter and rub it into
the dry ingredients, either by hand or using a
freestanding mixer.

In a separate bowl whisk the egg with the milk
and yoghurt. Make a well in the centre of the
flour and butter mixture and pour in the egg
mixture, stirring briefly until just combined
(it will be very sticky). Using a dough scraper or
spatula, transfer the dough to the lined baking
tin and level it out. Score a 2.5-cm-/1-inch-
deep cross into the top of the dough with a
sharp knife and dust lightly with flour.

Bake in the oven for 50 minutes to an hour
until the bread is deep brown and sounds
hollow when tapped on the bottom. Turn out
and cool on a wire rack.

Sharing Platters

Some might disagree, but we are wholehearted believers in sharing food. Whenever we go out for dinner, the three of us never order the same dish. Ordering is a protracted process as we democratically decide upon our three favourite dishes to be passed around the table and shared. As sisters, we have such similar tastes in food that we can order for each other, only occasionally forgetting about idiosyncrasies such as Nichola's mild allergy to scallops, Linsey's hatred for eggs and Gillian's dislike of tomato ketchup (catsup). In the past, new boyfriends have been quite shocked by our 'your plate is my plate' approach to eating. Those who didn't embrace it did not last long!

Visiting Barcelona on a family holiday as teenagers was such a revelation for us. We discovered a style of eating designed to be shared and, even better, served in small portions, allowing nine dishes to be tasted instead of just three. We still love the Spanish and Mediterranean approach to eating and try, whenever possible, to carry it over to our café menu. When we're catering for weddings and events, we always encourage people to consider sharing platters or family-style food service. If it were up to us, every meal would be served tapas style.

Many of our favourite food memories can be traced back to a great sharing platter (a good glass of wine also helps). During a tour of New Zealand a few years ago, Gillian and Nichola spent a perfect afternoon cycling between vineyards in the Marlborough region, tasting the famous Sauvignon Blanc and enjoying simple platters of olives, cold meats and cheeses to soak up the alcohol. It is fair to say the cycle home was a slow and wobbly one!

The key to a great sharing platter is simplicity. They are one of the easiest ways to put on a great spread at short notice. We have included a number of our most popular platter items but if you don't have time to make a homemade pesto or pâté then a simple spread of great, fresh produce from a farmers' market or quality supermarket will do just as nicely.

GILLIAN

Seafood Platter

This seafood board is our most popular sharing platter at the café.
Of course, the beauty of a platter is that you can mix and match
as you please, but ours consists of:

SMOKED MACKEREL PÂTÉ (page 130)
GOOD-QUALITY SMOKED SALMON
FIERY PRAWNS (below)
ROCKET, TO GARNISH · HOMEMADE MAYO (page 131)
HOMEMADE OATCAKES (page 88) OR IRISH SODA BREAD (page 122)
A WEDGE OF LEMON

Fiery Prawns

As well as being an essential part of the Seafood
Platter, these prawns make a really good, quick
pasta dish. Toss some pasta in olive oil, mix
through some chopped cherry tomatoes and top
with the prawns. LINSEY

SERVES 4

10 g (⅓ oz) unsalted butter
2 teaspoons extra virgin olive oil
20 raw shelled king prawns
1 red chilli (chile), finely diced (seeded if you
   prefer less heat)
grated zest of 1 lime, and juice of ½ lime
1 tablespoon roughly chopped fresh coriander
   (cilantro)

Heat the butter and oil in a shallow frying pan
on a high heat until the butter is foaming.

Fry the king prawns in the pan for 2 minutes,
stirring them occasionally.

After 2 minutes, add the chilli, lime zest and
juice and cook for a further two minutes.

Immediately remove from the pan, toss
through the coriander and serve.

Smoked Mackerel Pâté

This recipe is easy peasy and involves no more than throwing all the ingredients into a food processor and blending! It makes a lovely lunch snack served with oatcakes. NICHOLA

SERVES 4–6

250 g (9 oz) smoked mackerel fillets
200 g (7 oz/¾ cup) full-fat cream cheese
grated zest of 1 unwaxed lemon, and juice
   of ½ lemon
2 tablespoons creamed horseradish
3 tablespoons roughly chopped
   flat-leaf parsley

Debone and flake the mackrel fillets – the biggest bones lurk along the backbone, down the central line of the fillet (don't worry about tiny bones).

Put the deboned mackerel flakes in the bowl of a food processor. Add the remaining ingredients and pulse to combine, stopping when the pâté still has a rough texture.

Homemade Mayo

I'm not going to lead you in a merry dance and claim that Hellman's and Heinz don't play a big part in my precious condiments shelf. I'm a good stones-throw away from being the domestic goddess who can live without jarred goods. But, when (a little) time allows it is SO worth making your own mayo. It is worlds apart from its shop-bought friend, and is the perfect accompaniment to seafood. Try the alternative flavourings below, which make it suitable for almost any meat or fish. Tiny baby steps towards domestic goddessry indeed. LINSEY

MAKES ENOUGH TO FILL A STANDARD-SIZED JAM JAR (370 g/12½ oz)

1 large egg yolk, at room temperature
½ teaspoon Dijon mustard
½ teaspoon salt
¼ teaspoon white pepper
½ teaspoon caster (superfine) sugar
½ tablespoon white wine vinegar
150 ml (5 fl oz) vegetable oil and olive oil mixed (half and half)

Put the egg yolk, mustard, seasoning, sugar and 1 teaspoon of the vinegar in the small bowl of a food processor, fitted with the small blade. Blend on the fast setting for two minutes, or until the mixture turns pale and smooth.

Start to add the oil, a drop at a time, with the food processor still running. The mixture will get lighter in colour and become thick and silky.

When you have added half of the oil, begin adding slightly more each time – a teaspoon at each addition (if you add it any quicker, the mixture will split).

When all the oil has been added, stir to check the consistency. If it seems a little thick, add a teaspoon of hot water and pulse to combine. Continue to add hot water, a teaspoon at a time, until the mayonnaise has thinned down sufficiently. Now add the remaining vinegar and stir through with a spoon.

Transfer the mayonnaise to a clean jar or airtight container and store in the fridge. As it contains no preservatives or additives, use within four days of making.

OPTIONAL ADDED FLAVOURS
Fresh herbs and grated lemon zest – *great with white fish*

Sun-dried tomatoes and fresh basil – *perfect with simple roast chicken*

Capers and diced red onion – *ideal as a dip for bread, crisps or crudité*

Fresh chipotle chillies and lime zest – *see the recipe for Halloumi and Chipotle Mayo Mini Cornbread Sandwich on page 23*

Blue cheese and sautéed leek – *perfect with barbecued steak*

Ploughman's Platter

As a huge cheese-lover, the Ploughman's is my favourite platter.
We serve it in the café with a homemade chicken liver parfait, but
here we have Scotch eggs – a perfect picnic snack as they
are so transportable. GILLIAN

Our Ploughman's picnic contains:
SCOTCH EGGS (below) · MATURE CHEDDAR CHEESE
BRIE · HOMEMADE TOMATO CHUTNEY (page 136)
CHUNKS OF HOME-BAKED SOURDOUGH (page 117)

Scotch Eggs

Although there is a bit of work involved in home-
made Scotch eggs, the end result is so much more
satisfying than a shop-bought version. Bring them
along to a picnic and you'll be the most popular
person at the park, beach or bench. GILLIAN

MAKES 6

2 teaspoons vegetable oil
1 leek, topped and tailed, rinsed and
    finely chopped
1 white onion, finely chopped
2 garlic cloves, crushed
6 sage leaves, roughly chopped
1 teaspoon cumin seeds
1 teaspoon fennel seeds
1 kg (2 lb 3 oz) pork sausagemeat
1 teaspoon sweet-smoked paprika
6 large eggs, soft boiled, plus 2 large eggs,
    beaten
plain (all-purpose) flour, for dusting and rolling
100 g (3½ oz/1 cup) dried breadcrumbs

Heat the oil a shallow frying pan and on a
medium heat sauté the leek, onion and garlic
for 5–10 minutes. Stir frequently to prevent
them from over-browning. When the vegetables
are soft, remove from the heat and stir through
the sage.

While the vegetables are cooling, put a dry
frying pan on a high heat. Toast the cumin and
fennel seeds for 3–4 minutes, tossing regularly,
until golden and aromatic. Let the seeds to
cool, then grind to a fine sand-like texture with
a mortar and pestle or spice grinder. When
the vegetable mixture is cool, mix it with the
sausagemeat, smoked paprika and ground
seeds.

Dust the soft boiled eggs with a little flour.
On a large square of cling film, roll out a circle
of pork mixture about 15 cm (6 in) in diameter
and ½ cm (¼ in) thick. Place an egg in the
centre of the circle, then use the cling film
to wrap the pork all around the egg. Twist the
cling film to secure tightly. Do this with the
remaining 5 eggs.

Chill the eggs for half an hour to make them easier to handle. Preheat the oven to 180°C (350°F/Gas 4).

Take the eggs from the fridge and remove the cling film. Place a few tablespoons of flour in a shallow bowl, and the beaten eggs and breadcrumbs in 2 separate shallow bowls.

Roll the pork-covered eggs in the flour, then dip them in the beaten egg, then transfer to the breadcrumbs to coat all over.

Put on a lightly floured baking sheet and bake in the oven for 40 minutes, until the breadcrumbs are golden brown and the sausagemeat is cooked.

Homemade Tomato Chutney

This chutney is an excellent accompaniment to a ploughman's board as it goes well with pâté, ham or a good mature Cheddar cheese. My favourite is Isle of Arran Cheddar, but any good strong cheese will do. NICHOLA

MAKES ENOUGH TO FILL 2–3 STANDARD-SIZED JAM JARS

550 g (1 lb 2½ oz) Granny Smith apples
550 g (1 lb 2½ oz) soft, ripe tomatoes, quartered and cores removed
350 g (12 oz) white onions, quartered
250 g (9 oz) dried apricots, finely chopped
3 garlic cloves, finely sliced
350 g (12 oz/2 cups) soft, light brown sugar
¼ tablespoon cayenne pepper
¾ tablespoon ground ginger
1 teaspoon salt
850 ml (1½ pints) clear malt vinegar
15 g (½ oz) pickling spice

Quarter and core the apples (leave the skin on). Put the tomatoes, apples and onions in the large bowl of a food processor and whizz until the mixture is finely chopped but not pulped. Place the chopped mixture in a deep heavy-based pan. Add the chopped apricots, garlic, sugar, cayenne pepper, ginger, salt and vinegar.

Put the pickling spice in the centre of a square of thin, clean uncoloured fabric (we use muslin/cheesecloth). Gather the edges up around the spices and tie with a piece of string to form a little bag. Put the bag in the pan.

On a high heat bring the pan to a boil, then immediately turn down the heat. Simmer the chutney, uncovered, for 3–4 hours, stirring every half an hour. The chutney should be thick with no watery residue and should taste sharp, but not overpoweringly vinegary.

Allow to cool fully before serving. It will keep well in an airtight jar in a cool place for up to a month.

Mezze Platter

This is the type of platter which perfectly suits a sunny evening with a glass of chilled white wine. We often use red onion and aubergine for the roasted veg. GILLIAN

Our Mezze Platter consists of the following components:
HUMMUS (below) · GOOD-QUALITY OLIVES
MARINATED FETA (page 140) ·
HOME-BAKED FLATBREAD (page 118) · DUKKAH (page 141)
TZATZIKI (page 140) · ROASTED VEGETABLES

Hummus

This is such a staple in our lunchtime lives. It's simple and cheap to make and it is a completely different creature from the shop-bought equivalent. I love it without any additions as I find the subtle flavours of sesame and lemon a perfect blend, but try our optional added flavours for extra enhancements to make it a very different dish. LINSEY

SERVES 6

240 g (8½ oz) can of chickpeas (garbanzo beans), drained and rinsed
30 g (1 oz) light tahini paste
60 ml (2½ fl oz) extra virgin olive oil
2 small garlic cloves, crushed
grated zest and juice of ½ unwaxed lemon
a generous pinch of salt

Place all the ingredients in a food processor and blend until smooth. Taste for seasoning.

OPTIONAL ADDED FLAVOURS:
Dukkah (page 141)

Chopped fresh basil leaves and toasted, flaked almonds

Red chilli (chile) and fresh coriander (cilantro) leaves

Smoked paprika

Marinated Feta

Feta is such a delicious, salty cheese that it works well on a mezze platter straight out of the packet but taking the time to prepare this rosemary marinade will add an extra zing, making it well work the effort. GILLIAN

SERVES 4–6

3 garlic cloves
250 g (9 oz) feta cheese, cut into bite-sized
    chunks
1 sprig of mint, roughly chopped (including
    the stalk)
1 sprig of rosemary, leaves picked
4 tablespoons extra virgin olive oil
½ teaspoon cracked black pepper

Preheat the oven to 200°C (400°F/Gas 6).

Leaving the garlic cloves in their skin, wrap them in a piece of silver foil, and place on a baking tray. Roast in the oven for 15 minutes (this softens the garlic and makes it taste sweeter and milder). Remove the garlic from the oven and foil, and crush slightly using the back of a fork.

In bowl, combine the crushed garlic (discarding the skin), feta chunks, mint, rosemary leaves, oil and pepper. Leave to infuse at room temperature for a few hours before serving.

Tzatziki

No mezze platter would be complete without a traditional tzatziki dip to complement and cool the warm Eastern spices. GILLIAN

SERVES 4

¼ cucumber, cut into small dice
½ celery stick, cut into small dice
300 g (10½ oz/2½ cups) natural yoghurt
2 tablespoons roughly chopped mint leaves
1 teaspoon sea salt
a pinch of coarsely ground black pepper

Combine all the ingredients together in a bowl.

Ideally, leave to chill for an hour in the fridge before serving to allow the flavours to settle and amalgamate.

Dukkah

Dukkah is the most versatile of mezze accompaniments. It is a traditional Egyptian aromatic nut and seed side dish which can be used as a dip or garnish for just about any Middle Eastern-inspired recipe. I love to dip flatbread in olive oil followed by dukkah to maximise the amount captured!
GILLIAN

100 g (3½ oz/¾ cup) hazelnuts, without skins
100 g (3½ oz) sesame seeds
30 g (1 oz) cumin seeds
30 g (1 oz) coriander seeds
10 g (⅓ oz) fennel seeds
½ teaspoon hot paprika
1 teaspoon caster (superfine) sugar
½ teaspoon salt
½ teaspoon coarsely ground black pepper

Preheat the oven to 180°C (350°F/Gas 4).

Roughly pulse the hazelnuts in a food processor. You want them to remain fairly chunky, so be light-handed with the pulsing.

In a deep roasting tin, combine the hazelnuts, sesame, cumin, coriander and fennel seeds. Transfer to the oven for 15 minutes to toast. Remove the tin every 4–5 minutes and give them a shake so they don't burn. They should be fragrant and evenly browned.

Leave the nut and seed mixture to cool.

Finally, mix the paprika, sugar, salt and pepper through the nut and seed mixture. The dukkah will keep for up to 3 months in an airtight container at room temperature.

Kids Picnic Platter

'Picnic' is a time-honoured childhood feast for me. When I was a wee girl, my best friend's mum, Mary, would offer us sandwiches (or 'picnic') every time I was at her house. Picnic involved little more than a selection of chopped up vegetables, cheese and bread or toast but we found it the most entertaining of meals. What a sneaky way to get fruit and veg into your little ones! NICHOLA

Our kids platter features:
HUMMUS (page 137) · CARROT BATONS
CHEDDAR CHEESE CHOPPED INTO SOLDIERS · CUCUMBER STICKS
TOAST SOLDIERS FOR DIPPING
SLICES OF APPLE · RAISINS

Dinner

Anyone who has served time in the hospitality industry will tell you that, despite the long hours, the tough conditions and screaming chefs, one of the main draws is the feeling of being part of a family. I have never felt this so literally as I do at Three Sisters Bake. In addition to getting to work with my sisters every day, the team we have built across the kitchen and front of house feels very much part of our extended family now.

This is a feeling which we try to extend to our guests in the café. In the evening, the ambience of the café changes completely with fairy lights, candles, cocktails and great live music to complement our Soul BBQ menu. Since we launched our dinner menu, we have found that the informal, comforting, Americana-style food has excited our chefs and captured our customers' interest.

From our pulled pork, now a staple of many menus around town (ours is often reputed to be the best!), to the chicken in homemade barbecue sauce, every one of our Soul Food dishes has to be bold, satisfying and make you feel happy. We've included a couple of Soul Food dishes in this chapter and a few family meals, which are quick and easy to prepare at the end of a long day.

Peering out of the kitchen window on one of our Soul BBQ nights is always a kick for me. The café is full to bursting: people have travelled from all over, through winding country roads to our sleepy little village, coming together to enjoy good company, great live music and, of course, outstanding food.

LINSEY

Lime and Chilli Prawns with Coconut Rice

I use the slightly unconventional measure of a 225 g (8 oz) teacup for the coconut rice in this recipe. I have a vintage china teacup in my kitchen cupboard at home which I have discovered makes just the right amount of rice for two people. NICHOLA

SERVES 2

FOR THE PRAWNS
2 tablespoons sesame oil
1 cm (½ in) piece of ginger, finely chopped
grated zest and juice of 1 lime
½ red chilli (chile), seeded and finely chopped (keep seeds if you like an extra kick)
1 garlic clove, crushed
1 teaspoon brown sugar
12 raw shelled king prawns
1 red (bell) pepper, halved, stalk removed, seeded and cut into thin strips
20 g (¾ oz) bunch of coriander (cilantro), leaves and stalks roughly chopped
⅓ cucumber, cut into thin, 5-cm- (2-in-) sticks

FOR THE COCONUT RICE
1 teacup (225 g/8 oz/1 generous cup) white basmati rice, rinsed and soaked in tepid water for up to an hour
1 teacup (225 ml/8 fl oz/1 generous cup) coconut milk
1 teacup (225 ml/8 fl oz/1 generous cup) cold water

Mix the sesame oil, ginger, lime zest and juice, chilli, garlic and sugar in a bowl and add the prawns. Leave to marinate while you prepare the rice and garnish.

Pour the rice, coconut milk and water into a medium saucepan, stir and bring to the boil, uncovered, on a high heat. Turn down the heat, cover with a lid, and cook gently for 12 minutes until the rice is tender.

Remove the pan from the heat and leave it to stand, with the lid on, for 5 minutes.

Remove the prawns from the marinade. Heat a large frying pan or wok on a medium heat and fry the prawns for 3–4 minutes until they turn pink. Add the strips of pepper and cook for a further 2 minutes.

Remove the lid from the rice and use a fork to separate the grains (it should still be a little sticky). To serve, divide the rice between 2 bowls, top with the cooked prawns then garnish with the chopped coriander and cucumber.

Pork Wellington

Christmas is utterly my favourite time of year. As a family it is the one day that we are quite fierce about our traditions: there must be Disney and there must be a wellington – this is the pork variety. LINSEY

SERVES 6

2 kg (4½ lb) boned loin of pork
20 g (¾ oz) unsalted butter
1 teaspoon olive oil
1 eating apple, peeled, cored and cut into small dice
4 big sticks of rhubarb, tough strings removed if necessary, cut into small dice
½ teaspoon mixed spice
6 fresh sage leaves, finely chopped
150 g (5 oz/1½ cups) dried breadcrumbs
6 slices of Parma ham
500 g (1 lb 2 oz) ready-rolled all-butter puff pastry
1 large egg, beaten
flour, for dusting
salt and freshly ground black pepper

Slice the pork about three-quarters of the way through along the length of the loin. Score smaller slits parallel to the long deep slice to allow you to flatten the pork out a little further. Leaving the pork cut-side up, cover it with cling film and beat it with a rolling pin a few times to flatten it. Season the cut side.

Heat the butter and oil in a frying pan on a medium heat. Add the diced apple and rhubarb and sauté for 5 minutes, stirring regularly, until brown. Add the mixed spice, chopped sage and season then cook for a further 5 minutes. Set aside to cool.

Once completely cool, combine the rhubarb and apple mixture in a large bowl with the

breadcrumbs and mix well. Place the stuffing mixture in a line down the centre of the flattened pork loin to form a narrow mound.

Lift one of the edges of the pork loin and wrap it over the top of the stuffing to fully contain it. You should end up with a big roll of pork and stuffing. Wrap tightly in cling film and put in the fridge to chill for 20 minutes.

Preheat the oven to 200°C (400°F/Gas 6).

Lay the Parma ham slices on a large sheet of cling film, side by side. Unwrap the chilled pork and place it on top of the ham. Wrap the ham around the pork, with the help of the cling film, then discard the cling film.

Lay the puff pastry on a clean, floured surface. Place the Parma ham-wrapped pork in the middle of the pastry. Pull the nearest edge of pastry up and over the pork. Now roll the pork until it is fully wrapped in pastry. Seal the edges with egg wash and cut off any excess.

Dust a roasting tin with flour. Place the pork in the tin, seam side facing down, and brush it all over with egg wash. Make a couple of little incisions in the pastry to release the steam.

Bake in the oven for 15 minutes, then reduce the temperature to 180°C (350°F/Gas 4) and cover the pork with foil. Cook for a further 10 minutes, until the pastry is golden brown, then remove from the oven and leave it to rest for 10 minutes with the foil on. Remove the foil before slicing. Serve hot with a creamy sauce like rhubarb and ginger or apple.

Pete's Pulled Pork

We serve this recipe (our head chef Pete's), either as it is, with chilli corn-on-the-cob and collard greens or on Focaccia (page 112) as a sandwich. However it's served, it captures all the soul of the Deep South and we've never heard a bad word said against it. GILLIAN

SERVES 8

FOR THE HOUSE RUB
2 tablespoons smoked hot paprika
2 tablespoons ground cumin
2 tablespoons ground coriander
2 tablespoons ground cinnamon
a pinch of salt and freshly ground black pepper

FOR THE PULLED PORK
2 kg (4½ lb) boneless pork shoulder
2 white onions, roughly chopped
3 carrots, roughly chopped
2 celery sticks, roughly chopped
3 garlic cloves, crushed
600 ml (1 pint) hot beef stock
440 ml (15 fl oz) beer (bitter)
2 × 400 g (14 oz) tins of chopped tomatoes
3 sprigs of oregano
200 g (7 oz/⅚ cup) soft, dark brown sugar
300 ml (10 fl oz) cider vinegar
250 ml (8½ fl oz/1 scant cup) fresh orange juice

Preheat the oven to 240°C (460°F/Gas 8) or as high as it will go.

Combine all the house rub ingredients in a bowl then liberally rub into the pork.

Mix the chopped onions, carrots, celery and garlic in a bowl and spread in an even layer on the base of a deep roasting tin. Place the pork on the chopped vegetables, transfer to the oven and roast for 40 minutes.

Remove the pork from the oven and add the stock, beer, tomatoes and oregano. Turn the oven temperature down to 160°C (320°F/Gas 2). Cover the tin with foil, seal tightly and return the pork back to the oven to braise for 6 hours.

Remove the pork from the oven, uncover, take out of the roasting tin (reserving the juices), and allow to cool and rest a little before pulling the pork into shreds using forks or your fingers.

To make the barbecue sauce, pour the reserved juices or stock from the roasting tin into a large saucepan. Add the brown sugar, cider vinegar and orange juice. Simmer on a medium-high heat, uncovered, for 20–30 minutes until it has reduced by a third and is thick and smooth. Strain through a sieve.

Add the pulled pork to the sauce and stir to coat. Serve warm with fresh focaccia and rocket.

Sunshine Chicken

This is just one of my own Monday night, short-of-time, trying-to-reign-it-in-after-the-extravagances-of-the-weekend kind of meals. It's super-easy and simple to make. I love to serve it with sweet potato wedges baked with sea salt. Sunshine, summer, happy food. LINSEY

SERVES 4

4 skinless chicken breasts (approx. 150–200 g/ 5–7 oz each)
20 sun-dried tomatoes in oil, drained and cut into thin strips
grated zest of 2 unwaxed lemons
4 tablespoons roughly torn basil leaves
250 g (9 oz) tub of ricotta cheese
1 teaspoon sea salt
½ teaspoon coarsely ground black pepper

Preheat the oven to 190°C (375°F/Gas 5).

Cut a deep slit into the side of each chicken breast. You want to create a little pocket into which you can stuff the filling but don't cut all the way through to the other side.

In a bowl, combine the sun-dried tomatoes with the lemon zest, basil, ricotta and seasoning. Stuff each chicken breast with a quarter of the ricotta mixture, being careful not to overfill them, as you need to seal them shut.

Thread a cocktail stick back and forth between the open sides of each chicken breast to 'sew' it shut. This stops the ricotta mixture from escaping as it heats up.

Place the stuffed chicken breasts in a deep, lightly greased roasting tin. Cover the tin with foil and bake for 20–25 minutes, until the chicken is cooked through.

Camembert Fondue

We sisters have much in common. One of our favourite activities while we were growing up was, and still is, skiing. I'll be honest with you, ski holidays for us are 70 per cent about the snow and slopes, and 30 per cent about the abundance of melted cheese. This recipe is inspired by traditional fondue nights. It is a ridiculously easy starter or canapé alternative – sharing at its finest and simplest. LINSEY

SERVES 4

1 whole small Camembert, in its box
2 garlic cloves, sliced
a glug (30 ml/1¼ fl oz) of dry white wine
crusty bread, such as baguette, torn into
    chunks, to serve

Preheat the oven to 180°C (350°F/Gas 4).

Unwrap the Camembert from the plastic packaging and place it back in its cardboard box (with the lid off). Place on a baking sheet.

Make little incisions in the cheese with a sharp knife and slot a slice of garlic into each incision. Drizzle the cheese with the white wine and bake in the oven for 20–25 minutes until it feels soft.

Dip in crusty bread chunks and enjoy this melted cheese feast!

Swanky Mac and Cheese

This is the ultimate comfort food. With tweaks here and there, this recipe can be adapted to suit all tastes. In the café we follow the recipe below, adding a wholegrain mustard kick, but to make it child-friendly, omit the mustard to make it richer, substitute half the Cheddar for an Applewood cheese or smoked alternative. For devoted carnivores we add crispy fried cubes of pancetta. LINSEY

SERVES 4–6

EQUIPMENT:
Large oven proof baking dish or smaller
individual dishes

50 g (2 oz) salted butter
50 g (2 oz/³⁄₅ cup) plain (all purpose) flour
850 ml (1½ pints) semi-skimmed milk
200 g (7 oz) mature Cheddar cheese, grated,
    plus 50 g (2 oz) for the topping
½ tablespoon wholegrain mustard
½ teaspoon salt
a pinch of white pepper
250 g (9 oz) macaroni

Melt the butter in a heavy-based pan on a medium heat. Add the flour and stir immediately with a wooden spoon to combine. Cook the flour and butter for 2 minutes, stirring constantly, until the mixture (the roux) takes on a nutty, biscuity smell.

Gradually start adding the milk, a little at a time, stirring well after each addition. The flour mix will become very thick at this point.

Continue gradually adding the milk, stirring, until all the milk is incorporated into the roux (adding the milk slowly prevents lumps in the sauce).

Cook for 5–10 minutes, stirring, until you have a white sauce with a custardy consistency. Add a little more milk if it is too thick, then remove the pan from the heat.

Add the cheese to the white sauce and stir for a few minutes until the cheese has thoroughly melted. Finally add the mustard, salt and pepper. Add further seasoning to taste, if you like.

Preheat the oven to 180°C (350°F/Gas 4).

Cook the macaroni in a large pan of boiling salted water, according to the packet instructions. Drain the macaroni, return it to the pan, then stir in the cheese sauce. Tip the macaroni into an oven-proof baking dish.

Top with the remaining grated cheese and bake for 20 minutes.

Chicken and Ham Hock Pie

This delicious pie is a real wintery treat. Ham hocks are one of the tastiest and cheapest ingredients you will find, making it a great budget-friendly meal. GILLIAN

SERVES 4

EQUIPMENT:
20 × 25 cm (8 × 10 in) pie dish, roughly
    5 cm (2 in) deep

1 smoked ham hock (500 g/1 lb 2 oz), rinsed
3 juniper berries
2 bay leaves
3 garlic cloves, crushed
1½ teaspoons olive oil
50 g (2 oz) unsalted butter
4 skinless chicken thigh fillets (approx. 600 g/
    1 lb 3 oz in total), flesh sliced into thick strips
1 white onion, diced
2 leeks, trimmed, rinsed and diced
1 small carrot, diced
3 sprigs of fresh thyme
2 tablespoons plain (all-purpose) flour
300 ml (10 fl oz) semi-skimmed milk
15 g (½ oz) tarragon leaves, roughly chopped
150 g (5 oz) ready-rolled puff pastry
1 large egg, beaten
salt and freshly ground black pepper

Place the ham hock in a large pan, cover with water and add the juniper berries, bay leaves and 2 of the crushed garlic cloves. Bring to the boil and simmer gently, uncovered, for 4 hours or until the meat is soft and falling from the bone. Remove the ham from the pan, set aside to cool, and retain the stock.

Heat the oil and butter in a wide heavy-based pan on a medium-high heat. Add the chicken strips and cook until they are browned on the outside. Add the onion, leeks, carrot, the remaining clove of garlic and thyme and fry for 5 minutes, stirring frequently, until the vegetables are soft and golden.

Preheat the oven to 200°C (400°F/Gas 6).

Add the flour to the chicken and vegetables and cook, stirring, for 2–3 minutes. Add the milk a little at a time, stirring well between additions, then add 150 ml (5 fl oz) of the reserved ham stock, stirring continuously for 5–10 minutes on a low heat until thickened.

Shred the meat from the ham hock and add it to the pan, along with the tarragon, and season. Cover and cook on a low heat for 2 minutes.

Transfer the chicken and ham mix to the pie dish. Lay the puff pastry over the top of the filling, pressing the edges of the pastry onto the pie dish and cut off any excess pastry.

Use a very sharp, small knife, to cut two leaf shapes from the leftover pastry. Mark the leaves with little lines and place on the top of the pie. Brush the pastry with egg wash and bake for 15 minutes or until the pastry is golden brown.

Yoghurt, Mint and Rosemary Marinated Lamb

These kebabs are crying out to be served with our Watermelon, Feta and Mint Salad (page 44). LINSEY

SERVES 4

EQUIPMENT:
8 wooden or metal skewers

FOR THE MARINADE
150 g (5 oz/scant ⅔ cup) natural yoghurt
juice of 1 lemon
1 tablespoon olive oil
1 garlic clove, crushed
a pinch of salt and freshly ground black pepper
2 sprigs of mint, stalks and leaves finely chopped
12 sprigs of rosemary, leaves picked and roughly chopped

1 kg (2 lb 3 oz) fillet end of leg or lamb neck fillet, cut into bite-sized chunks
lemon wedges, to serve
homemade Flatbread (page 118), to serve
Raita (page 99), to serve

Combine the marinade ingredients in a large bowl. Add the lamb chunks and mix well. Cover the bowl with cling film and leave to marinate in the fridge overnight.

If using wooden skewers soak them in cold water for 10 minutes. Thread the lamb onto the skewers.

Cook the kebabs on a barbecue for 10 minutes (for medium-cooked lamb), turning frequently. Alternatively, heat a teaspoon of olive oil in a non-stick griddle pan on a high heat. Cook the skewers for 5–8 minutes, turning frequently.

Serve with lemon wedges, flatbread and raita.

Dad's Barbecue Glaze

This is a barbecue staple in our house. It's also one of the two 'dishes' that Dad can make – the other being scrambled eggs! You can marinate anything in this – pork chops, chicken thighs, homemade beef burgers, pork and herb sausages. They are all really good with this glaze spread evenly over them an hour or so before throwing on to the barbecue.

LINSEY

MAKES ENOUGH TO FILL ONE STANDARD-SIZED JAM JAR (370 g/12½ oz)

100 ml (3½ fl oz) rapeseed or vegetable oil
100 ml (3½ fl oz) tomato ketchup (catsup)
1 tablespoon Worcestershire sauce
1 heaped teaspoon English mustard powder
50 g (2 oz/¼ cup) soft, light brown sugar
a generous pinch of salt and freshly ground
    black pepper

Combine all the ingredients in a large bowl.

Store in an airtight jar and chill until ready to use. It keeps well for up to 1 month.

Fish in Parcels

Another very quick dish to throw together when you're in a rush. You're really just steaming the fish in its own juices and some lovely added flavours. Do play around with different combinations – I constantly do, but these are two recipes which I return to again and again. LINSEY

SERVES 2

2 white fish fillets or fish loins (sustainably caught cod, haddock or sole)

FOR THE CREAMY FENNEL FISH PARCEL
1 small red onion, very thinly sliced
2 teaspoons roughly chopped tarragon leaves
30 ml (1 fl oz) dry white wine
2 tablespoons crème fraîche
½ fennel bulb, trimmed and shaved into thin slices
sea salt and freshly ground black pepper

FOR THE SPICY THAI FISH PARCEL
1 fresh red chilli (chile), seeded and finely sliced
½ stick lemongrass, sliced lengthways into very thin strips
3 teaspoons roughly chopped coriander (cilantro)
juice of 1 lemon
200 ml (7 fl oz) coconut milk
½ teaspoon sea salt

Preheat the oven to 170°C (335°F/Gas 3).

Lay 2 large squares of greaseproof (wax) paper or foil on a flat surface. Place a fillet or loin of fish on each. Choose one of the parcel recipes and divide the ingredients equally between each piece of fish – bring the edges of the paper or foil up around the fish pieces to prevent the liquid escaping – and season.

Seal the parcels by pulling the edges of the paper or foil up and folding them together. Foil is very easy to just fold, squeeze and seal but you may need to tie paper parcels with string. Make sure they are well-sealed as you don't want all the steam and juices to escape.

Place the parcels side by side in a deep roasting tin and bake for 10–15 minutes, depending on the thickness of the fillet or loin. If in doubt, check the fish after 10 minutes as the worst thing you can do to tender white fish is overcook it.

Life-saver Ice Cubes

Since becoming a mum, I've tried to become one of those organised types who has handy cooking aids in the freezer to cut down prep time for various dishes. I know Lins also swears by these as she became fed up buying a vast number of ingredients like lemongrass and coconut milk, only for the remainder of the stalk or can to go off. NICHOLA

Lemongrass, Chilli, Lime and Coconut Milk Cubes

Great added with chicken or prawns for a Thai curry or stir fry.

MAKES 20 ICE CUBES

1 stick of lemongrass
2 red chillies (chiles), seeded, or seeds left
  in for a kick
400 ml (14 fl oz) tin of coconut milk
grated zest of 3 limes

Finely chop the lemongrass and chillies. Mix with the coconut milk and zest.

Divide between 20 cubes and freeze.

Garlic and Herb Oil Cubes

These add flavour and depth to sauces, or can be melted in a pan before frying a steak.

MAKES 10 ICE CUBES

10 garlic cloves, crushed
10 g (⅓ oz) flat-leaf parsley, finely chopped
10 g (⅓ oz) fresh oregano, finely chopped
150 ml (5 fl oz) extra virgin olive oil

Mix all the ingredients together thoroughly. Pair into 20 cubes and freeze.

Lemon, Olive and Sun-dried Tomato Cubes

Melt these through cooked pasta and add parmesan and fresh herbs to make a super-quick dinner.

MAKES 6 ICE CUBES

150 g (5 oz) sun-dried tomatoes in oil, finely chopped (retain oil)
grated zest of 3 unwaxed lemons
100 g (3½ oz) chopped black olives, pitted in brine

Combine the sun-dried tomatoes with their oil, the lemon zest and olives. Divide the mixture between 6 cubes. Top up with a little extra virgin olive oil to fill the cubes if needed. Freeze.

Pesto Cubes

Defrost and drizzle over cooked chicken or fork through pasta.

See Basil Pesto recipe on page 175

Leftover pesto can be transferred to as many cubes as needed and frozen for a later date.

Caramelized Onion Cubes

It is important to freeze the onion marmalade when it's been freshly made (and cooled).

See Red Onion Marmalade recipe on page 34

These cubes freeze really well and can be removed in small portions and defrosted to top canapés, fill quiches or used in scrambled eggs with toasted pine nuts (pine kernels) (page 34). It is delicious when defrosted in a sandwich with brie.

Kids Chicken Dippers with Homemade Salsa

You can guarantee clean plates with this. I have worked with a lot of families and have spent hours putting together something I deemed child-friendly that would go down like a lead balloon. This was always a good dish to serve the next night to win back the kids' affection and my own self confidence. LINSEY

MAKES 10–12 DIPPERS

FOR THE CHICKEN DIPPERS
75 g (2½ oz/¾ cup) dried breadcrumbs
1 small 50 g (2 oz) packet of plain salted
   crisps (chips), crushed into small pieces
   in the bag
50 g (2 oz/½ cup) plain (all-purpose) flour
1 large egg, beaten
2 boneless and skinless chicken breasts, cut
   into strips (5–6 strips per breast) or 500 g
   (1 lb 2 oz) packet of chicken mini fillets

FOR THE SALSA
400 g (14 oz) tin of chopped tomatoes
grated zest of 1 lime
1 tablespoon finely chopped coriander (cilantro)
1 tablespoon soft, light brown sugar
a dash of balsamic vinegar
a pinch of salt

Preheat the oven to 180°C (350°F/Gas 4).

Mix the breadcrumbs and crisps together in a large bowl. Place the flour and egg in 2 separate shallow bowls.

Toss the chicken strips in the flour to coat. Dip the floured chicken pieces one by one in the beaten egg, then coat in the breadcrumb and crisp mixture. Transfer the coated chicken strips to a deep roasting tin and bake for 15–20 minutes, until the chicken is cooked through.

Meanwhile, prepare the salsa. Strain the chopped tomatoes through a sieve. Discard the juices. Combine the tomatoes with the remaining salsa ingredients and stir well.

Serve the chicken dippers with the salsa and a salad or some steamed vegetables (there's only a mild reduction in likeable factor by adding veg!).

Basil Pesto

Another simple child-friendly classic. This is the key to getting children past their fear of green food. To sneak extra goodness into it, and therefore them, add a handful of fresh spinach or kale too – they won't know the difference. Trickery, but for a good cause! This is one thing I now won't eat from a jar – homemade pesto is far tastier, has no artificial additives and is ready at the touch of a button. LINSEY

150 g (5 oz) fresh basil leaves
100 g (3½ oz) parmesan cheese, grated
2 garlic cloves
100 g (3½ oz) toasted pine nuts (pine kernels)
½ teaspoon coarsely ground black pepper
juice of 1 lemon and grated zest of ½ unwaxed
  lemon
400 ml (14 fl oz) olive oil
a generous pinch of salt

Whizz all the ingredients in a food processor for 1 minute until the pesto becomes coarse in texture.

Store in the fridge in an airtight container for up to a week.

Cakes

and

Sweet

Treats

As a child, my favourite book was Roald Dahl's *George's Marvellous Medicine*. I would spend hours creating colourful lotions, potions and mixtures. Emptying the contents of Mum's old-fashioned pantry and syphoning teaspoons of spices, flour, treacle, food colouring and whatever else I could lay my hands on.

My interest in potion making gradually evolved into a love of baking. I would sit on the work surface while Mum or Granny baked; breaking eggs, weighing out ingredients, stirring the mixing bowl and, of course, licking the wooden spoon. As a home economics teacher, our Mum was only too delighted to watch as her middle daughter's aptitude for domestic science blossomed!

In school, my interests lay in the world of science. I was delighted when I started high school and discovered that Chemistry was actually just a continuation of the potion making and experimentation of my childhood. I went on to study Chemistry at university and then to work for a pharmaceuticals company. All the while, I remained a keen baker and would frequently be found whiling away a Sunday afternoon scientifically measuring the ingredients for an upside down peach cake into my prized pink Kitchen Aid mixer!

After making a huge batch of cupcakes as a gift for a friend's wedding, it occurred to me that I enjoyed baking WAY more than my corporate job. I began investigating ways to start my own baking business from home and secured a start up Business Gateway grant. I used the grant very carefully, buying stock, marketing flyers, cake boxes and cake stands. Using a website I designed myself and working from my kitchen table, I launched my fledgling wedding cake business which, three years later, would evolve into Three Sisters Bake.

NICHOLA

'Naked' Victoria Sponge Wedding Cake

This beautiful summery wedding cake will wow your guests. It needs to be as fresh as possible (ideally made the day before) so unless you want to be knee-deep in flour the day before your wedding speak nicely to a friend or relative who enjoys baking. It is an 'all-in-one' sponge recipe so fairly quick to make however, it's not a cake that should be rushed.

NICHOLA

SERVES 60–80

EQUIPMENT:
1 or 2 × 12 cm (5 in) loose bottomed cake tin(s)
1 or 2 × 18 cm (7 in) loose bottomed cake tin(s)
1 or 2 × 25 cm (10 in) loose bottomed cake tin(s)
1 or 2 × 32 cm (13 in) loose bottomed cake tin(s)

In total you will be making 12 layers of sponge cake so you will need to make the cakes in three batches. If you have 2 of each size of tin, you will be able to prepare the next batch of cake mix as the previous batch is baking. Don't worry if you don't, it will just take a little longer to bake the cakes. You will end up with a 4-tier cake with 3 cake layers in each tier.

TOTAL SPONGE CAKE INGREDIENTS
880 g (1 lb 13 oz/7 cups) self-raising flour
880 g (1 lb 13 oz/4 cups) caster (superfine) sugar
880 g (1 lb 13 oz) unsalted butter, softened, plus extra for greasing
16 large eggs, at room temperature
8 teaspoons baking powder
8–10 drops vanilla extract

FOR EACH BATCH OF CAKES
220 g (8 oz/1 cup) self-raising flour
220 g (8 oz/1 cup) caster (superfine) sugar

220 g (8 oz) unsalted butter, softened, plus extra for greasing
4 large eggs, at room temperature
2 teaspoons baking powder
2–3 drops vanilla extract

FOR THE BUTTERCREAM
400 g (14 oz) unsalted butter, softened
1 kg (2 lb 3 oz/8½ cups) icing (confectioners') sugar, plus extra for dusting
150–200 ml (5–7 fl oz) whole (full-cream) milk

30 dessertspoons raspberry jam (ideally homemade)
fresh flowers and assorted berries (such as blueberries, raspberries and strawberries), to garnish

Preheat the oven to 160°C (320°F/Gas 2). Grease one of each size of tin and line the base and sides with greaseproof (wax) paper.

Place all the ingredients (the batch quantities as listed opposite) in a freestanding mixer (or mix in a large bowl with an electric hand mixer) and beat for 2–3 minutes until the mixture is fluffy and lighter in colour.

Divide the mixture between the 4 tins, placing progressively smaller amounts of the mixture into the decending sizes of cake tin. There should be a relatively thin layer of cake mix in each. Don't worry too much about the exact quantities going into each – part of the charm of this cake it its rustic look. Smooth out the surface of the cake mix in the tins before baking.

The 2 smaller tins should fit on one rack in the oven. Bake for 20–25 minutes until springy to touch. Allow the cakes to cool in the tins a little, then turn out onto a wire rack.

Repeat this process until you end up with 12 layers of cake (3 layers per tier).

To make buttercream, place the butter and icing sugar in a freestanding mixer and beat until very light and fluffy (alternatively, mix in a large bowl with an electric hand mixer) – this can take up to 5 minutes. Pour in the milk slowly, adding enough to ensure the icing is soft and easy to spread.

Take your first 32 cm (13 in) sponge cake and put it on a large cake board. On the top-side, spread a thin layer of raspberry jam followed by buttercream. Sandwich the next 32 cm (13 in) layer on top. Repeat this once more. Do not put jam and buttercream on the top layer. Repeat this step with the 25 cm (10 in), 18 cm (7 in) cakes and 12 cm (5 in) cakes. You should end up with 4 stacks of cakes.

Using a palette knife, carefully lift the 25 cm (10 in) tier and stack it on top of the 32 cm (13 in) tier. Then lift the 18 cm (7 in) tier and stack it on top of the 25 cm (10 in) tier. Finally lift the 12 cm (5 in) tier and stack it on top of the 18 cm (7 in) tier.

Decorate the cake with fresh flowers and berries and finish with a dusting of icing sugar.

Photograph overleaf

Raspberry and Coconut Cake

Our Raspberry and Coconut Cake has the nostalgic quality of a classic Victoria Sponge (page 180) with a contemporary coconutty twist. It is an easy peasy cake to make in a rush but still has 'wow factor'. If you want to make it really special, dress it up with white chocolate scrolls around the side and a topping of fresh raspberries. It's so pretty, I even baked one for my own wedding cake table! NICHOLA

SERVES 8–10

EQUIPMENT:
2 × 23 cm (9 in) round loose-bottomed cake tins

225 g (8 oz/ scant 2 cups) self-raising flour
2 teaspoons baking powder
225 g (8 oz) unsalted butter, softened or at room temperature, plus extra for greasing
225 g (8 oz/1 cup) caster (superfine) sugar
4 large eggs, at room temperature
75 g (2½ oz/¾ cup) desiccated coconut
3 tablespoons (45 ml/2 fl oz) tinned coconut milk

FOR THE BUTTERCREAM
375 g (13 oz/3 cups) icing (confectioners') sugar
130 g (4½ oz) unsalted butter, softened or at room temperature
4 tablespoons (65 ml/2½ fl oz) tinned coconut milk

5 dessertspoons of raspberry jam (ideally homemade)
fresh raspberries, to garnish
toasted coconut flakes, to garnish

Preheat the oven to 160°C (320°F/Gas 2).

Grease the sides of the cake tins and line the base with greaseproof (wax) paper.

Sift the flour and baking powder into a large bowl, or the bowl of a freestanding mixer. Add the butter, sugar and eggs and beat all the ingredients together for 2–3 minutes until the mixture is smooth and pale. Beat the desiccated coconut and coconut milk into the cake mixture. If using a freestanding mixer, turn it down to slow speed before adding the coconut.

Divide the mixture evenly between the 2 prepared cake tins and smooth the tops. Bake for 25–30 minutes until evenly golden and springy to the touch. Allow the cakes to cool in the tins a little, then turn out onto a wire rack.

To make the buttercream, sift the icing sugar into a bowl and add the butter (alternatively, use a freestanding mixer). Beat for 3–5 minutes until very light and fluffy. Slowly pour in the coconut milk and beat until smooth. If the icing seems a little stiff add one more tablespoon of coconut milk.

To assemble the cake, spread the top of one sponge cake with the raspberry jam then top with just less than half the icing. Sandwich the other sponge on top and spread the remaining icing on top. Place the fresh raspberries in a 'crown' around the top of the cake and sprinkle the middle with toasted flakes of coconut.

Chocolate Splodge

*This is one of the simplest recipes in the book. It needs no cooking,
so is great fun to make with kids. Mum used to make this with us on rainy
school holiday days (they were relatively frequent growing up in the west
of Scotland!). Mum named it 'splodge' and the name has stuck.
Younger visitors to the café love it.* NICHOLA

MAKES 16–20 BARS

EQUIPMENT:
24 × 34 cm (9½ × 13 in) baking tin

550 g (1 lb 2½ oz) digestive biscuits
275 g (10 oz) unsalted butter
275 g (10 oz) good-quality dark chocolate
  (50-60% cocoa solids), broken into pieces
275 g (10 oz/generous 2 cups) raisins
300 g (10½ oz) condensed milk
500 g (1 lb 2 oz) good-quality milk chocolate

Line the base and sides of the tin with grease-proof (wax) paper.

Place the digestive biscuits in a large bowl and smash them into small pieces with the end of a rolling pin.

Melt the butter and dark chocolate in a heat-proof bowl set over a pan of simmering water (making sure that the bottom of the bowl does not touch the water), stirring occasionally. Once melted, remove the bowl from the pan and stir in the raisins and condensed milk. Fold the broken biscuits into chocolate mixture and stir until all the biscuit pieces are incorporated.

Press the mixture into the tin, making sure to press it into all the sides and corners. Try to get it as flat and even as possible. Place in the fridge for 20–30 minutes to set.

Melt the milk chocolate in a heatproof bowl set over a pan of simmering water and pour it over the 'splodge', spreading it even and neatly. Put it back in the fridge for 20–30 minutes until set. Cut the splodge into bars and dig in!

Ginger Crunch

I discovered this moreish gingery treat in Australia. I spent weeks trying to perfect a recipe on my return to Scotland, to no avail. I was eventually put out of my misery when Gillian's sister-in-law, Yvonne, visited with a batch of ginger crunch tasting just like the Australian treat I had been trying to recreate. Luckily, Yvonne was happy to share her recipe, which is now a staple café sweet treat – thanks Yvonne. NICHOLA

MAKES 16–20 BARS

EQUIPMENT:
24 × 34 cm (9½ × 13 in) baking tin

FOR THE SHORTBREAD BASE
280 g (10 oz/2¼ cups) plain (all-purpose) flour
125 g (4½ oz/generous ½ cup) caster (superfine) sugar
1½ teaspoons baking powder
2½ teaspoons ground ginger
180 g (6 oz) cold unsalted butter, cubed, plus extra for greasing

FOR THE FUDGY GINGER TOPPING
180 g (6 oz) unsalted butter
100 g (3½ oz) golden syrup (dark corn syrup)
375 g (13 oz/3 cups) icing (confectioners') sugar
2½ teaspoons ground ginger

Preheat the oven to 180°C (350°F/Gas 4).

Line the base of the baking tin with greaseproof (wax) paper and butter the sides.

To make the shortbread base, place the flour, sugar, baking powder and ginger in a food processor and pulse briefly to mix the ingredients. Add the butter and pulse until the mixture resembles coarse breadcrumbs. Alternatively, mix the dry ingredients in a large bowl and rub in the butter by hand.

Press the mixture firmly into the prepared tin, leveling it out using a spatula. Bake for 18 minutes, until the shortbread is golden brown. Remove the tin and set aside to cool.

For the topping, place the butter and syrup in a pan and melt on a very low heat (or in a microwave). Sift the icing sugar and ground ginger into the melted butter and syrup mix. Beat the mixture with an electric hand mixer until it is thick and fudgy looking.

Pour the topping over the shortbread and spread it out evenly with a spatula. Allow to set before cutting into bars.

Chocolate Orange Cake

This is a truly decadent cake... one for the grown ups. The cooking process really maximizes the zesty flavour of the oranges, giving this cake a real distinctive citrussy ZING! The recipe is flourless so, although it's not entirely gluten-free, it is suitable for those with a mild gluten intolerance. NICHOLA

SERVES 8–10

EQUIPMENT:
23 cm (9 in) round loose-bottomed cake tin

3 oranges
6 large eggs, at room temperature
250 g (9 oz/generous cup) caster (superfine) sugar
200 g (7 oz) ground almonds
1 teaspoon baking powder
½ teaspoon bicarbonate of soda (baking soda)
60 g (2 oz) cocoa powder

FOR THE GANACHE
200 g (7 oz) good-quality dark chocolate, broken into pieces
130 g (4½ oz) unsalted butter
1 teaspoon golden syrup (dark corn syrup)
50 ml (2 fl oz) double (heavy) cream

Place the whole oranges in a large pan and cover with cold water. Place on a medium-high heat and bring to the boil. Cover the pan, turn down the heat and simmer for 2 hours, checking occasionally that the water has not evaporated. Remove from the heat, drain the oranges and set aside to cool.

Once the oranges are cool, cut them into quarters, remove the pips and place the orange quarters, skin and all, in a food processor. Blitz until you have a relatively smooth orange pulp.

Preheat the oven to 180°C (350°F/Gas 4).

Line the base and sides of the cake tin with greaseproof (wax) paper.

Beat the eggs and sugar in a large bowl for 1–2 minutes until well combined. Add 375 g (13 oz) of the blitzed oranges and mix (if there is any remaining orange you can freeze it for next time). Then add the ground almonds, baking powder, bicarbonate of soda and cocoa powder and stir, making sure all ingredients are well combined.

Pour the mixture into the prepared tin and bake in the oven for 50 minutes, or until a skewer inserted into the centre of the cake comes out clean. Allow the cake to cool in the tin a little, then turn out onto a wire rack.

To make the ganache, melt the chocolate and butter with the syrup in a heatproof bowl set over a pan of simmering water (making sure that the bottom of the pan does not touch the water), stirring occasionally.

Remove from the heat and leave to cool a little before stirring through the cream.

Pour the warm ganache over the cake and let it drizzle down the sides of the cake. Allow 30 minutes for it to set before serving.

Nectarine and Raspberry Cake

The ground almonds in this cake give it a lovely moist texture. You can replace the nectarines with apples or plums (you'd need 5 or 6 plums) depending on the time of year or occasion. NICHOLA

SERVES 8–10

EQUIPMENT:
23 cm (9 in) round loose-bottomed cake tin

180 g (6 oz) unsalted butter, softened
180 g (6 oz/generous ¾ cup) caster (superfine) sugar
1 teaspoon vanilla extract
3 large eggs, at room temperature
100 g (3½ oz) ground almonds
150 g (5 oz/1¼ cups) self-raising flour, sifted
3 ripe nectarines, stoned and cut into 1-cm- (½-in-) thick slices (unpeeled)
handful of fresh raspberries
handful of flaked almonds
icing (confectioners') sugar, for dusting

Preheat the oven to 175°C (350°F/Gas 4).

Line the base and sides of the cake tin with greaseproof (wax) paper.

Beat the butter, sugar and vanilla extract in the large bowl of a freestanding mixer or with an electric hand mixer until pale and creamy, then beat in the eggs, one at a time. Fold the ground almonds and flour into the mixture until combined.

Spoon and spread enough of the cake mixture into the tin to cover the bottom (a bit less than half). Lay the nectarine slices and raspberries on the mixture.

Spoon and spread the remaining cake mixture over the top of the fruit. Don't worry if the fruit pokes out of the mixture here and there.

Scatter the flaked almonds over the top and bake in the oven for 45–50 minutes, until the cake is golden brown and a skewer inserted into the middle of the cake comes out clean.

Remove from the oven and leave to cool in the tin. Once cooled, dust with a little icing sugar.

Apple, Almond and Coconut Cake

This lovely moist cake is a great gluten-free treat and, providing gluten-free baking powder is used (available in large supermarkets), it is suitable for coeliacs. NICHOLA

SERVES 8–10

EQUIPMENT:
20 cm (8 in) round loose-bottomed cake tin

2 eating apples peeled, cored and diced
grated zest of 1 unwaxed lemon,and juice
    of ½ lemon
6 large eggs, at room temperature
225 g (8 oz/1 cup) caster (superfine) sugar
240 g (8½ oz) ground almonds
1 teaspoon gluten-free baking powder
½ teaspoon vanilla extract
40 g (1½ oz/½ cup) flaked almonds
handful of flaked coconut shavings
    (alternatively use desiccated coconut)

FOR THE COCONUT BUTTERCREAM
280 g (10 oz/2⅓ cups) icing (confectioners')
    sugar
100 g (3½ oz) unsalted butter, softened, plus
    extra for greasing
3 tablespoons (50 ml/2 fl oz) coconut milk

Place the diced apples in a pan with the lemon juice and zest and cook on a low heat, covered, for 15–20 minutes until softened. Set aside to cool.

Preheat the oven to 160°C (320°F/Gas 2).

Line the base and sides of the tin with grease-proof (wax) paper.

Whisk the eggs and sugar together in a large bowl until light and pale, then stir in the cooled, cooked apples. Add the ground almonds, baking powder, vanilla extract and flaked almonds and stir until all ingredients are well combined.

Pour the cake mixture into the prepared tin and bake in the oven for 40 minutes, until a skewer inserted into the middle of the cake comes out clean. If the skewer comes out sticky with cake mixture, give the cake another 10 minutes in the oven. Remove the cake and set aside to cool in the tin.

To make the buttercream, whisk the icing sugar and butter together for 5 minutes, until light and fluffy. Add the coconut milk and whisk for another minute.

Once the cake has cooled, turn it out of the tin and top it with the buttercream. Finally, sprinkle with coconut shavings.

Courgette *and* Lime Cake

We each have a few favourite cakes and menu items in the café and Courgette and Lime Cake is definitely one of Gillian's. She campaigned to have this recipe added to our café repertoire in the face of protest from myself and Linsey that it sounded very strange and nobody would order it! It does indeed sound rather strange but give it a try and you will learn why Gillian loves it so much. NICHOLA

SERVES 8–10

EQUIPMENT:
20 cm (8 in) round loose-bottomed cake tin

FOR THE CAKE
135 ml (4½ fl oz) sunflower oil
200 g (7 oz/⅘ cup) caster (superfine) sugar
3 large eggs, at room temperature
300 g (10½ oz/2½ cups) self-raising flour
½ teaspoon bicarbonate of soda (baking soda)
1 teaspoon baking powder
335 g (11¾ oz) finely grated courgette (zucchini)
grated zest of 2 limes

FOR THE ICING (FROSTING)
200 g (7 oz/generous ¾ cup) full-fat cream cheese
100 g (3½ oz/generous ¾ cup) icing (confectioners') sugar
grated zest and juice of 1 lime

courgette ribbons, to decorate

Preheat the oven to 160°C (320°F/Gas 2).

Line the base and sides of the cake tin with greaseproof (wax) paper.

Beat the oil, sugar and eggs together in a large bowl with an electric hand mixer for 2–3 minutes, until light and fluffy. Sift in the flour, bicarbonate of soda and baking powder and fold into the mixture. Fold in the grated courgette and lime zest.

Pour into the prepared tin and bake for 40–50 minutes, until golden brown and a skewer inserted into the middle of the cake comes out clean. Allow the cake to cool a little in the tin, then turn out onto a wire rack.

To make the icing, beat the cream cheese and icing sugar together until smooth. Add the lime zest and juice and stir.

Once cool, top the cake with the icing by running a spatula or palate knife back and forth over the cake creating deep grooves to give a nice textural look.

Note: *courgette ribbons make a great decoration but remove before eating.*

Lemon and Blueberry Cake

*This cake is a regular guest in our cake cabinet and has proved hugely
popular. With a heaped topping of blueberries, it makes a beautiful and
mouthwatering centrepiece for a special event or afternoon tea.*

NICHOLA

SERVES 8–10

EQUIPMENT:
20 cm (8 in) round loose-bottomed cake tin

FOR THE CAKE
180 g (6 oz) unsalted butter, softened or at
　　room temperature
225 g (8 oz/scant 2 cups) self-raising flour, sifted
180 g (6 oz/generous ¾ cup) caster
　　(superfine) sugar
3 large eggs, at room temperature
1 teaspoon baking powder
1 teaspoon vanilla extract
60 ml (2 fl oz) crème fraîche
grated zest of 2 unwaxed lemons
large punnet (300 g/10½ oz) of blueberries

FOR THE ICING (FROSTING)
150 g (5 oz/scant ⅔ cup) full-fat cream cheese
75 g (2½ oz/generous ½ cup) icing
　　(confectioners') sugar, plus a little extra
　　for dusting
grated zest and juice of 1 unwaxed lemon

Preheat the oven to 160°C (320°F/Gas 2).

Line the base and sides of the cake tin with
greaseproof (wax) paper.

Place the butter, flour, sugar, eggs, baking
powder and vanilla extract in a large bowl
and beat with an electric hand mixer for a few
minutes until the mixture is light and fluffy.
Add the crème fraîche and lemon zest and
beat the mixture for another 30 seconds. Stir
through 2 handfuls of the blueberries.

Pour the mixture into the prepared tin and
bake for 40–50 minutes until golden brown.
Test to see if the cake is cooked by inserting a
skewer into the middle of the cake. If it comes
out clean, the cake is cooked. If not bake for a
few more minutes.

To make the icing, beat the cream cheese and
icing sugar together until smooth. Add the
lemon zest and juice and stir through.

Remove the cake from the oven and allow to
cool a little in the tin, then turn out onto a wire
rack. Once the cake has cooled, spread the icing
on top, scatter over the remaining blueberries
and dust with icing sugar.

Giant Empire Biscuits

Empire biscuits, previously known as Linzer biscuits or German biscuits, were renamed after the outbreak of World War I as a patriotic gesture. In spite of their origin, Scotland firmly adopted this shortbread jam sandwich and they can still be found in any village or high street bakery across the country. Our versions are giant but remain true to the original – topped with a glacé cherry. GILLIAN

MAKES 12

225 g (8 oz) unsalted butter, softened
100 g (3½ oz/scant ½ cup) caster (superfine) sugar
250 g (9 oz/2 cups) plain (all-purpose) flour, sifted, plus extra for dusting
good-quality raspberry jam
450 g (1 lb/3 ½ cups) icing (confectioners') sugar
60 ml (2 fl oz) whole (full-cream) milk
glacé cherries (or jelly tots), to decorate

Preheat the oven to 180°C (350°F/Gas 4).

Line 2 baking trays with baking parchment.

Beat the butter with the sugar in a large bowl for 2–3 minutes with an electric hand mixer until light and fluffy. Add the flour and mix very briefly until just combined.

Roll the dough out onto a lightly floured surface until it is about 5 mm (¼ in) thick. Cut the dough into circles using a plain round cookie cutter. You should be able to get 24 round shapes from the dough.

Place the shapes on the lined baking trays – 6 per tray – and bake for 8–10 minutes until the biscuits are lightly golden. You will need to bake the biscuits in two batches.

Allow the biscuits to cool on the baking trays for 5 minutes before transferring them to a wire rack to cool completely.

Dollop a teaspoon of raspberry jam onto the underside of a biscuit, spreading it out a little but not right to the edges, then sandwich a second biscuit on top (underside on the jam). Repeat with the remaining biscuits.

Using a small whisk, mix together the icing sugar and milk to form a spreadable icing. Spread the icing on top of the biscuit sandwiches using the back of a teaspoon, then top each one with half a glacé cherry or a jelly tot while the icing is still wet.

Coconut and Custard Pie with Passionfruit Curd

This pie is a regular feature on our Soul BBQ evening menu. Tasked with developing a number of Americana-inspired dessert recipes, our baker, Dave, delivered a few delights including this delicious coconut and custard pie. GILLIAN

SERVES 12

EQUIPMENT:
25 cm (10 in) loose-bottomed fluted tart tin
    baking beans

FOR THE PASTRY
235 g (8 oz/scant 2 cups) plain (all-purpose)
    flour, plus extra for dusting
50 g (2 oz/¼ cup) caster (superfine) sugar
150 g (5 oz) unsalted butter, chilled and cubed
1 large egg, at room temperature

FOR THE COCONUT FILLING
250 g (9 oz/generous cup) caster
    (superfine) sugar
100 g (3½ oz) unsalted butter, softened
2 large eggs, at room temperature
200 g (7 oz/2 cups) desiccated coconut
250 ml (9 fl oz) whole (full-cream) milk
60 g (2 oz) condensed milk
1 teaspoon vanilla extract
15 g (½ oz) plain (all-purpose) flour

passionfruit curd, to serve (page 214)

To make the pastry, place the flour and sugar in a food processor and pulse briefly to mix. Add the butter bit by bit and pulse until the mixture resembles breadcrumbs. Add the egg and pulse until the pastry starts to come together.

Turn the dough out onto a lightly floured surface and knead briefly. Shape it into a ball, wrap in cling film then chill for 1–2 hours.

Preheat the oven to 180°C (350°F/Gas 4).

Remove the pastry from the fridge, take off the cling film and allow to sit for 10–20 minutes to warm up a little. Lightly flour the surface and your rolling pin and roll the pastry out until it is 5 mm (¼ in) thick or large enough to line the tin.

Drape the pastry over the rolling pin and ease it into the tin, pressing it gently into the edges. Roll the rolling pin over the top of the tin to trim off excess pastry. Prick the base of the pastry a few times then place greaseproof (wax) paper into the case, fill with baking beans and bake for 20–25 minutes until golden brown. Remove from the oven, take out the paper and beans, and set aside to cool. Turn the oven temperature down to 170°C (335°F/Gas 3).

To make the filling, beat the sugar and butter together until pale and fluffy. Continue beating while you add the eggs, one at a time. Add the remaining ingredients and beat well to combine. Carefully pour the coconut filling into the pastry case and bake for 25 minutes until golden brown and no longer wobbly.

Remove from the tin and turn out onto a wire rack to cool. Serve with passionfruit curd.

Chocolate Brownies

These scrummy brownies are a hit with the kids in the café. Make them a little more grown-up by adding cherries to the mix or serving with fresh cherries and cream.

MAKES 16–20 BROWNIES

EQUIPMENT:
24 × 34 cm (9½ × 13 in) baking tin

225 g (8 oz) unsalted butter, plus extra for greasing
225 g (8 oz) good-quality dark chocolate (we use 53% cocoa solids Belgian chocolate chips)
4 large eggs, at room temperature
325 g (11 oz/scant 1½ cups) caster (superfine) sugar
100 g (3½ oz/scant cup) plain (all-purpose) flour
50 g (2 oz) cocoa powder
50 g (20 oz) fresh cherries, optional

Preheat the oven to 160°C (320°F/Gas 2).

Grease and line the base and sides of the tin with greaseproof (wax) paper.

Melt the butter and chocolate in a heatproof bowl set over a pan of simmering water (making sure that the bottom of the bowl does not touch the water). Stir occasionally until the butter and chocolate have melted. Remove the bowl from the pan and set aside to cool slightly.

Beat the eggs and sugar in a large bowl with an electric hand mixer for about 5 minutes, until thick, glossy and pale. Pour the cooled chocolate and butter into the egg and sugar mixture and gently fold it in until well combined. Sift the flour and cocoa powder over the mixture and fold it in.

Spoon the brownie batter into the prepared tin. Ease the mixture into the corners and level it out with a spatula. Bake for 30 minutes. If the brownie still has a wobble to it after 30 minutes, give it another 5 minutes in the oven. Once ready the brownie should look shiny and papery on top.

Cut into even-sized pieces and serve with fresh cherries.

Apple and Cherry Crumble

*On a cold, dark Scottish evening (of which there are many), there's
nothing like a warm crumble for pudding.*

SERVES 8

EQUIPMENT:
24 cm (9½ in) ovenproof pie dish

FOR THE FILLING
350 g (12 oz) cooking apples, peeled, cored
   and chopped
100 g (3½ oz) frozen dark cherries
50 g (2 oz/¼ cup) soft, light brown sugar
¼ teaspoon ground cinnamon
1 teaspoon vanilla extract

FOR THE CRUMBLE TOPPING
200 g (7 oz/1⅔ cups) plain (all-purpose)
   flour, sifted
a pinch of salt
200 g (7 oz) unsalted butter, chilled and cubed
100 g (3½ oz/1 cup) jumbo oats
175 g (6 oz/1 cup) soft, light brown sugar

Preheat the oven to 180°C (350°F/Gas 4).

To make the filling, place all the ingredients
in a pan and cook on a low heat for 5 minutes,
stirring occasionally, until the apples have
softened.

For the crumble topping, rub the flour, salt and
butter with your fingertips, in a large bowl, until
the mixture resembles coarse breadcrumbs.
Add the oats and sugar and stir to combine.

Transfer the cooked fruit to the pie dish
and top with the crumble topping. Bake for
20–25 minutes until golden brown.

Serve warm with vanilla ice cream or cream.

Dark Chocolate and Raspberry Tarts

We love food which looks as good as it tastes, and these dainty tarts certainly qualify in this category. They are so pretty, in fact, that we served them at an Alice in Wonderland-themed party we hosted at the café. Needless to say they went down a treat. GILLIAN

MAKES 8 TARTS

EQUIPMENT:
12-hole muffin tin
baking beans

1 × quantity of Coconut and Custard Pie pastry
   (page 202)
150 g (5 oz) good-quality dark chocolate,
   (50–60% cocoa solids)
100 g (3½ oz) unsalted butter, plus extra
   for greasing
1 large whole egg and 1 large egg yolk
30 g (1 oz/⅙ cup) caster (superfine) sugar
12 tablespoons homemade or good-quality
   raspberry jam
cocoa powder/icing (confectioners') sugar,
   for dusting
8 fresh raspberries, to decorate

Preheat the oven to 180°C (350°F/Gas 4) and grease the muffin tin.

Make the pastry as described on page 202. Chill in the fridge for 30 minutes then roll it out on a lightly floured surface until it is about 5 mm (¼ in) thick. Cutout 8 circles with a 9-cm- (3½-in-) round cookie cutter, and gently press the pastry circles into the greased muffin tin. Line each tart case with greaseproof (wax) paper, fill with baking beans and 'blind' bake for 15–20 minutes until the pastry is golden brown.

Remove the tin from the oven, take out the greaseproof paper and baking beans, and set aside to cool. Turn the oven temperature down to 170°C (335°F/Gas 3).

Melt the chocolate and butter in a heatproof bowl set over a pan of simmering water (making sure that the bottom of the bowl does not touch the water). Stir occasionally until the butter and chocolate have melted. Remove the bowl from the pan and set aside to cool slightly.

Using an electric hand mixer, whisk the egg, egg yolk and sugar in a large bowl until glossy, then fold the whisked egg mixture into the melted chocolate and butter mixture.

Put a tablespoon of jam into each baked tart case. Pour the chocolate mixture into the cases, right up to the top and bake in the oven for 5 minutes.

Remove from the oven and leave to cool, decorating with fresh raspberries before the chocolate has fully set, then dust with either cocoa or icing sugar.

Chocolate Brownie Milkshake

Who says milkshakes are just for kids? We're all for eating healthily Monday to Friday but there is just no point in counting calories when preparing a chocolate milkshake! Without the creamy goodness of the ice cream and the rich chocolatey flavour from the brownie, this recipe simply wouldn't work. If you don't believe us try it, it is utterly fabulous.

NICHOLA

MAKES 2 LARGE OR 6 SMALL MILKSHAKES

2 Chocolate Brownies (page 206), chopped
    or broken into chunks
400 ml (14 fl oz) whole (full-cream) milk
100 ml (3½ fl oz) double (heavy) cream
2 scoops of good-quality vanilla ice cream

Combine all ingredients in a blender or liquidizer and whizz until you reach the desired consistency – we like it quite smooth but with a few lumps of chewy brownie still intact. Pour into tall glasses and enjoy!

Lemon Curd

This classic recipe can be adapted to use the juice of most fruits, but it works particularly well with strong, sharp flavours like lemon, lime, orange or passionfruit. We serve lemon curd with our homemade scones in the café and passionfruit curd has become a big favourite on the dessert menu – we serve it with the Coconut and Custard Pie (page 202). NICHOLA

MAKES ENOUGH TO FILL A STANDARD-SIZED JAM JAR (370 g/12½ oz)

2 whole large eggs and 6 large egg yolks
225 g (8 oz/1 cup) caster (superfine) sugar
250 ml (9 fl oz) fresh lemon juice
pinch of salt
110 g (3½ oz) chilled unsalted butter, cut into cubes

Place the whole eggs, egg yolks, sugar, lemon juice and salt in a heatproof bowl, whisk to combine, then set the bowl over a pan of simmering water (making sure that the bottom of the bowl does not touch the water). Whisk constantly for 10–15 minutes, or until the mixture thickens and holds its shape when stirred.

Remove the bowl from the heat and stir in the butter. Once the butter has melted, strain the curd through a sieve into a metal bowl. Set the bowl over a bowl of iced water and stir occasionally for 5 minutes until cool.

Chill overnight. The curd can be kept in an airtight container in the fridge for up to 2 weeks.

Berry Compote

We wait all year for the Scottish berry season to come, then stress out about how to use the thousands of berries when we've gone overboard with picking. Berry compote is even nicer made with those berries that are just a little over-ripe, so can't be used elsewhere, but are too packed with flavour to waste. LINSEY

250 g (9 oz) caster (superfine) sugar
250 ml (9 fl oz) water
300–400 g (10–14 oz) mixed berries
  frozen or fresh)

Place the sugar and water in a heavy-based pan. Bring to the boil, continuously stirring until the sugar has dissolved. Turn the heat down and simmer for 5–10 minutes until the liquid looks syrupy.

Remove from the heat and stir through the mixed berries.

Allow to cool completely before using.

Acknowledgements

First and foremost thank you to Mum and Dad. Even though we know you would have preferred us to stay in 'sensible' jobs, we have no words to express our gratitude for your unwavering support over the past two years. We know our ideas can be harebrained. Thank you for steering us clear of the bad ones and encouraging us to fight tooth and nail for the good. It is truly a wonder the lengths you go to for us. Thanks also for helping us out on a daily basis and for not taking the phone off the hook, despite there always being a 50 per cent chance it will be a request for a dishwasher/babysitter/handyman/baking expert/courier!

Thank you to all our customers. We have been completely humbled by the sheer number of people who have travelled from near and far to visit our little village and sample our cakes, salads and pulled pork. Big thanks especially to our regular customers from Quarriers and the surrounding villages. Your familiar faces and the friendships we have formed over the last two years have been a truly unexpected privilege.

To all our staff, present and past, without a doubt there would be no Three Sisters Bake without you. We imagined we would run the café as a three-man band, a truly absurd thought now. Our original vision has been adapted and moulded around you guys and without your input, ideas, humour and energy, our café wouldn't be half the place it has become.

Special thanks to Jessica Statham, our first barista and manager. You answered our cry for help with your beautiful coffee skills, fantastic way with customers and staff and cheery face, even at the end of a 16-hour shift. You helped us to organise, systematise and generally find order in the midst of chaos! London has gained a fantastic new friend, we miss you.

To our Big Chef (Peter Wilson). God only knows where we'd be without you. We started our café with big dreams for our food. Your passion for big flavours, experimentation and competitive cook-offs on your days off have raised the bar further than we could have imagined. We see things coming out of our kitchen that make us burst with pride. Thank you.

For Clive and Douglas. Thank you for being such fantastic and supportive husbands/brother-in-laws! Thank you for understanding that being married to Nichola and Gillian also means being married to a café. Thank you for lending us your accounting, joinery and jewellery skills and for setting up wedding cakes, working behind our bar and picking up the pieces when things go wrong.

For all our friends, in particular, the dedicated DIY team – we owe a lot of people a lot of painting hours. Thank you all for turning up in your best overalls and slaving away. The homemade cakes began in those days for our break times and have continued ever since, only with a far prettier backdrop due to your handiwork. Thanks also for your support in visiting the café with your family and friends over the past two years, especially in the early days when we were afraid we'd have no 'real' customers!

Granny McCallum for being a fantastic granny, sweetie shop owner and tablet maker. We believe the hospitality gene has been passed to us from you. Not many kids get to grow up playing shops in a real life sweetie shop, thank you for helping to create such amazing childhood memories and for inspiring us to go on and open a sweetie shop of our very own!

Liz Tate, our very first mentor and customer service inspiration – ever a professional. Very few days pass at Three Sisters Bake without a 'What would Liz do?' moment.

Lisa Palompo Dixon of Palompo PR. For jumping onboard with our brand and 'selling' Three Sisters Bake with more enthusiasm and confidence than we could ever have managed alone. For not laughing at our biggest dreams... and then playing an integral part in them coming true.

Helen Cathcart, what you do with that camera we will never understand. You catapult every-day sights in to things of pure beauty, and have filled this book with just that.

Clare Skeats, because of your inspired design skills we have a truly beautiful book – beyond what we could have imagined.

Thanks to Hardie Grant and in particularly to Kate Pollard for taking a chance on us and believing that we would be able to produce a great book.

Finally, for each other. This would have been a horrendous and lonely solo journey. Where might we go on this rollercoaster next?

About the authors

Gillian, Nichola and Linsey Reith are a trio of self-confessed food fanatics with a strong catering pedigree and chef training behind them. As the daughters of a home economics teacher and granddaughters of a sweetie shop owner, they have risen through the ranks at some of Glasgow's most coveted eateries.

The girls were inspired by their global travels and love of good home-made food to open Three Sisters Bake, a café and craft boutique near Glasgow. The café serves a range of wholesome, high-quality, fresh, colourful homemade foods in a relaxed rural neighbourhood setting. It has been nominated for several awards.

Three Sisters Bake 2014 by Gillian Reith, Nichola Reith and Linsey Reith

First published in 2014 by Hardie Grant Books

Hardie Grant Books London
Dudley House, North Suite
34–35 Southampton Street
London WC2E 7HF
www.hardiegrant.co.uk

Hardie Grant Books (Australia)
Ground Floor, Building 1
658 Church Street
Melbourne, VIC 3121
www.hardiegrant.com.au

British Library Cataloguing-in-Publication Data. A catalogue record
for this book is available from the British Library.

ISBN 978-1-74270-676-4

Publisher: Kate Pollard
Desk Editor: Kajal Mistry
Editor: Laura Nickoll
Indexer: Cathy Heath
Cover and Internal design: Clare Skeats
Photography and retouching © Helen Cathcart
Colour reproduction: P2D
Cover retouching: Steve Crozier
Photography assistant: Faith Mason

Printed and bound in China by 1010 Printing International Limited

10 9 8 7 6 5 4 3 2 1